Unfinished Tasks: The New International Trade Theory and the Post-Uruguay Round Challenges

by F.M. Scherer and Richard S. Belous

Issues Paper No. 3

BRITISH-NORTH AMERICAN COMMITTEE
Sponsored by
British-North American Research Association (UK)
National Planning Association (USA)
C.D. Howe Institute (Canada)

©British-North American Committee
Quotations with appropriate credit permissible

ISBN 0-89068-126-0
Library of Congress Catalog Card Number 94-66903
Published by the British-North American Committee

Printed and bound in the United States

May 1994

To Barbara and Trace

Contents

Contents

Preface by the Joint Chairmen

The British-North American Committee has two goals in publishing this study. First, while we applaud the completion of the Uruguay Round of negotiations of the General Agreement on Tariffs and Trade (GATT), we believe that there are still many unfinished tasks in the area of international trade. Our first goal is to focus attention on the key issues that remain unresolved so that efforts to solve vexing trade matters are given a high priority.

Our second goal stems from the observation that economic theories concerning international trade, sometimes known as the "new international trade theory" (NITT) or, less frequently, "strategic trade theory," are moving from largely academic discussion to the actual development of trade policy.

Until now, most of the NITT literature has been written in technical language supported with econometrics not readily interpretable by laypeople. The second goal of this study is to present NITT in a way that allows informed readers to take part in the debate.

These two goals are crucially linked. Much of the unfinished business in the post-Uruguay Round era deals with nontariff trade barriers. However, NITT is significantly different from classical trade models in analysis of, and policy recommendations for, nontariff trade barrier issues. It tends to stress the importance of bilateral relations outside the context of GATT, and the acceptance of its validity would therefore put at risk much for which GATT stands.

To help the Committee appreciate the issues, we asked one of our members, Professor F.M. Scherer of the John F. Kennedy School of Government of Harvard University, and Dr. Richard S. Belous, the Committee's North American Director, to write this study. We endorse their conclusion: that there needs to be a renewed sense of urgency concerning the drafting of new rules for international trade that could decrease the likelihood of future trade distortions and trade warfare.

(Continued)

We urge our trade negotiators and other policymakers to consider the analysis and recommendations of this study, and we commend it to them and to all who are interested in opening up the international trading system.

SIR DAVID PLASTOW
Cochairman

JOHN G. HEIMANN
Cochairman

DAVID MORTON
Chairman, Executive Committee

Executive Summary

The next few years will be a critical period for international trade despite—and because of—the major achievements in 1993. The Uruguay Round agreement, between 117 General Agreement on Tariffs and Trade (GATT) signatory nations, was reached in December 1993. It contains many new provisions that move toward harmonizing world trading and investment relationships. Yet many of the Uruguay Round's initial goals were not accomplished.

The North American Free Trade Agreement (NAFTA)—which the U.S. Congress, the Canadian Parliament, and the Mexican legislature approved in 1993—now links the U.S., Canadian, and Mexican markets. However, the actual working of NAFTA will be determined by the day-to-day implementation decisions made over the next few years. Enlargement of the European Union will present similar challenges.

Thus, despite the accomplishments of 1993, there are many unfinished tasks. These have resulted partly from deliberate choice in eleventh-hour Uruguay Round and NAFTA compromises made to secure agreement. It remains to be seen, for example, what the new GATT rules concerning dumping really mean and how effectively a new World Trade Organization (WTO) will function. Even the name of the WTO was in doubt until the April 15, 1994, signing ceremony in Marrakesh. The original Uruguay Round agreement text called the new organization the Multilateral Trade Organization. However, after the formal talks, the U.S. team obtained tacit agreement from key negotiators to change the name to the WTO. The Clinton administration perceived that the word "world"—as opposed to "multilateral"—would play better in Washington. Nevertheless, much more than just the WTO's eventual name remains unclear. Despite the gains of the Uruguay Round, many services remain outside the revised GATT system, and some of the most important nontariff trade barriers are untouched.

This study seeks to illuminate the still unresolved issues of world trade. Its point of departure is the observation that economic theories concerning international trade have outrun world trading policies. In recent years a "new international trade theory" (NITT), also called "strategic trade theory," has been emerging. It differs in several crucial ways from classical models of international trade. The influence of NITT has extended well beyond academia, partly because some NITT theorists have become high level policy advisors in the United States and other countries, but also because nations and their national champion enterprises[1] have adopted the sophisticated trading strategies characterized by NITT. Nature is imitating art. As the influence of NITT spreads, it will have serious policy implications for public and private sector decisionmakers. Yet this is scarcely understood because most of the NITT literature is inaccessible to the layperson.

This study presents the major points of NITT in a way that allows informed readers to become involved in the debate. It traces the historical roots of NITT, showing that many of the ideas articulated by NITT contributors have existed in more primitive forms for nearly two centuries. It then explores the policy implications of NITT and the need to develop and adopt "new rules of the road" governing international trade—often in major nontariff barrier areas—in the next set of world trade discussions.

Findings

The basic conclusions of this study include the following:

1. Standard or classical theories of international trade often perform poorly in explaining and predicting the trade flows that occur.

2. The new international trade theory often seems to provide a better explanation of many ongoing events.

3. NITT focuses on phenomena such as economies of scale, technological innovation, research and development, product life cycles, intra-industry and intrafirm trading practices, human resource programs, foreign exchange policies, and monopolistic and/or oligopolistic behavior as key forces that can shape a nation's comparative advantage.

4. Unlike in the standard models of international trade, strategy plays a very important role in NITT. In other words, in the NITT paradigm, comparative advantage is something that is fought for and won, not merely inherited or revealed.

5. NITT models tend to support more activist government policies in international trade than classical models. Such activist policies differ in many ways from traditional protectionism.

---

1. A so-called national champion enterprise is one that is supported or encouraged by the state in an effort to promote national interests. Most often these national champions are in high technology industries.

6. NITT models highlight the importance of nontariff trade barrier issues such as investment strategies, control over distribution channels, intellectual property rights, tax policies, and other domestic policies that influence international trade.

7. NITT models and their advocates are already exerting a significant impact on public and private sector decisionmakers.

Unfinished Tasks

This study details the policy implications of NITT for governments, corporations, and labor unions. It emphasizes NITT's problems and potential costs as well as its benefits. One major problem is the likelihood of retaliation against nations that employ NITT strategies. Political realities also complicate the implementation of NITT strategies. Nevertheless, for better or for worse, NITT will have a growing influence on the way that world trade is conducted in the 1990s and beyond.

The Uruguay Round achieved significant progress. But many unfinished tasks remain. The spread of NITT thinking makes it all the more urgent to formulate new rules concerning dumping, nontariff barriers, investments, the environment, and many forms of government subsidy and promotion. The hope of the authors is that from a better understanding of NITT will come a renewed sense of urgency concerning the implementation of new rules of the road, which in turn will limit the likelihood of future trade distortions and trade warfare.

About the Authors

F.M. Scherer is Professor of Business and Government at the John F. Kennedy School of Government, Harvard University. He has also taught at Princeton University, the University of Michigan, Northwestern University, and Swarthmore College. From 1974 to 1976, he was Chief Economist of the Federal Trade Commission. His undergraduate degree was from the University of Michigan; he received his M.B.A. and Ph.D. from Harvard University. Professor Scherer's research specialties are industrial economics and the economics of technological change. He is the author of *Industrial Market Structure and Economic Performance* (with David Ross); *International High-Technology Competition; Mergers, Sell-offs and Economic Efficiency* (with David J. Ravenscraft); *Innovation and Growth: Schumpeterian Perspectives;* and *The Weapons Acquisition Process* (two volumes, one with M.J. Peck). His most recent research has focused on international competition policy. Professor Scherer is past President of the Industrial Organization Society and the International Joseph A. Schumpeter Society, Vice President of the American Economic Association, and Vice President of the Southern Economic Association.

Richard S. Belous is the North American Director of the British-North American Committee. He is also Vice President of International Programs and Chief Economist at the National Planning Association, which is the American sponsor of the Committee. Dr. Belous is an Adjunct Professor at George Washington University and lectures at the U.S. State Department's Foreign Service Institute. He was an economist with the Conference Board and the Congressional Research Service. He earned his B.A. from Columbia College and his M.A. and Ph.D. in economics from George Washington University. His primary areas of research include international economics and human resources. He is the author of *The Contingent Economy: The Growth of the Temporary, Part-Time and Subcontracted Labor Force; NAFTA as a Model of Development: The Benefits and Costs of Merging High and Low Wage Areas* (edited with Jonathan Lemco); and *The Growth of Regional Trading Blocs in the Global Economy* (edited with Rebecca S. Hartley). He has been an advisor to two U.S. presidential commissions.

1. Setting the Stage

The British economist John Maynard Keynes wrote:

> The ideas of economists and political philosophers, both when they are
> right and when they are wrong, are more powerful than is commonly
> understood. Indeed the world is ruled by little else. Practical men, who
> believe themselves to be quite exempt from any intellectual influences, are
> usually the slaves of some defunct economist. Madmen in authority, who
> hear voices in the air, are distilling their frenzy from some academic
> scribbler of a few years back. I am sure that the power of vested interests
> is vastly exaggerated compared with the gradual encroachment of ideas.
> Not, indeed, immediately, but after a certain interval; for in the field of
> economic and political philosophy there are not many who are influenced
> by new theories after they are 25 or 30 years of age, so that the ideas which
> civil servants and politicians and even agitators apply to current events are
> not likely to be the newest. But, soon or late, it is ideas, not vested interests,
> which are dangerous for good or evil.[1]

Keynes's observation is certainly correct in the field of international trade. The
views of Adam Smith, David Ricardo, Friedrich List, and other economists have
had a major impact on public and private sector decisionmakers—even those
who believe themselves to be exempt from intellectual influences.

In most debates, free trade is lauded as "a good thing," and protectionism is
seen as "a bad thing." This "classical" perspective, which traces its roots to
Adam Smith, gained credence when protectionist measures were found to
aggravate the Great Depression of the 1930s. Seeking not to repeat the errors of
the 1930s, the General Agreement on Tariffs and Trade (GATT), ratified in
1947, urged in its preamble that nations "enter . . . into reciprocal and mutually
advantageous arrangements directed to the substantial reduction of tariffs and
other barriers to trade and to the elimination of discriminatory treatment in
international commerce." In this way, it stated, nations' "relations in the field
of trade and economic endeavor should be conducted with a view to raising
standards of living, ensuring full employment and a large and steadily growing
volume of real income and effective demand, developing the full use of the
resources of the world and expanding the production and exchange of goods."

1

Those who favor protectionism in contravention of these broad GATT principles have often been on the defensive. They are charged with protecting a special interest and not with advancing the overall welfare of society or the global economy. Attacks on the classical economic models—and those contrived by their followers—have characteristically fallen short. Until a few years ago, alternative views did not carry the intellectual weight of the traditional models, at least not in English-speaking nations.

1.1   New Views

Recently, however, the traditional view has been challenged by a new paradigm that claims to do a better job of predicting and explaining international trade patterns. This "new international trade theory" (NITT)—also called "strategic trade theory"—emphasizes oligopolistic and monopolistic competition rather than perfect competition and phenomena such as economies of scale, technological innovation, research and development (R&D), and trading within firms and within industries. In doing so, NITT claims to provide a more realistic perspective on trading patterns, with important real-world policy implications for government, business, and labor. The new view of world trade often suggests policies at odds with those of traditional models.

Chapter 2 of this study describes the evolution and revolution taking place in economic thought. It begins by contrasting the standard views of world trade accepted in North America and Great Britain with the newer paradigm. Chapter 3 explores basic features of the new international trade theory and explains why the newer models look to unconventional variables to explain trade flows in global markets. Strategy, which plays a key role in the newer models, is investigated in Chapter 4. Chapter 5 considers a range of specific ways in which NITT policies can be, and are, implemented. Chapter 6 explores the need for new "rules of the road" in international trade and the future prospects of the new views concerning world trade.

Notes

1. John Maynard Keynes, *The General Theory of Employment, Interest, and Money* (New York, N.Y.: Harcourt, Brace, and World, 1936), pp. 383-384.

2. Evolution and Revolution in Economic Theory

Economists have long asked why nations trade and what determines the specific goods and services they exchange, as well as the equally important question of what should be the goals or benefits a nation hopes to secure through international trade. Two centuries ago, three different answers to these questions contended for support. They can be characterized, with only slight violence to their enormous complexity, as first, mercantilism; second, the free trade school originating with Adam Smith; and third, the national development school associated with Friedrich List.

When Adam Smith published his path-breaking *Wealth of Nations* in 1776, he launched a frontal attack on the then dominant strain of thought concerning international trade—the system known as mercantilism. The mercantilists perceived international trade as a kind of zero-sum game: if Nation A gained by accumulating a substantial trade surplus, its trading partner, Nation B, lost commensurately. A nation's goal in the trading arena, the mercantilists argued, should be to achieve a substantial export surplus and thereby accumulate a hefty stock of gold and silver—the principal monetary metals. Implicit or explicit in this belief was the assumption that nations had unemployed or underemployed resources, especially labor. Through tariffs and quotas that limited imports and subsidies for exports, outlets would be found for additional or surplus production, and the monetary metals accumulated through trading would stimulate domestic economic activity and hence employment. A second commonly shared objective was the use of international trade to build up a war chest to finance overseas adventures, and in that way to enhance national or royal power.

2.1 Comparative Advantage

Smith's *Wealth of Nations* was first and foremost a challenge to mercantilist principles. In his view, the main purpose of economic activity was to satisfy consumers' wants for goods and services, not to pile up unpalatable, unwearable metallic money hoards. Having shown that specialization in production and the exchange of goods and services made a nation's citizens more prosperous—a positive-sum game—he went on to apply the same logic to foreign trade:

3

> What is prudence in the conduct of every private family, can scarce be folly
> in that of a great kingdom. If a foreign country can supply us with a
> commodity cheaper than we ourselves can make it, better buy it of them
> with some part of the produce of our own industry, employed in a way in
> which we have some advantage.[1]

Thus emerged the famous law of comparative advantage, whose logic was articulated further in David Ricardo's *Principles of Political Economy* (1817) and many subsequent works by the so-called classical economists. The law of comparative advantage says that a nation should specialize in producing and exporting commodities it can produce at relatively low cost and that it should import those goods of which it is a relatively high cost producer. In the classical view, it was the force of comparative advantage in a free market system that governed actual international trading patterns.

A key assumption underlying this classical argument was that a nation's resources would be fully employed in any event. Therefore, they ought to be allocated toward the goods and services they supplied best, whether for domestic consumption or in exchange for other nations' output. To achieve the full advantages of international trade, Smith and his followers insisted, tariffs, quotas, bounties, and the like should be dismantled. During Smith's lifetime, this campaign was unsuccessful, and Smith spent the last 12 years of his life as Commissioner of Customs in Edinburgh, a surprising calling he is said to have pursued with vigor.

Ricardo's advocacy (among other positions, as a member of Parliament) was more successful. In 1828, Parliament weakened the Corn Laws that had traditionally protected British agriculture, and in 1846, as the Irish famine gathered momentum and other European grain supplies proved increasingly unreliable, Great Britain moved to an essentially free trade policy by repealing the last vestiges of the Corn Laws.

2.2   Nation Building

Meanwhile, a third school of thought was less eager to follow the free trade drummer. Jean-Baptiste Colbert, Finance Minister to King Louis XIV, strayed sufficiently from mercantilism in his attempts to build French industry that he is considered one of the third school's originators. More seminal to the founding of the third school, however, was Alexander Hamilton, the first Secretary of the Treasury of the newly independent United States. In his *Report on the Subject of Manufactures*, Hamilton insisted that:

Not only the wealth, but the independence and security of a Country, appear to be materially connected with the prosperity of manufactures. Every nation, with a view to those great objects, ought to endeavor to possess within itself all the essentials of national supply. These comprise the means of *Subsistence, habitation, clothing,* and *defence.*[2]

Because the British government had discouraged manufacturing in colonial America, Hamilton believed that American manufacturers suffered a substantial disadvantage in any competition "with those who have attained to perfection in the business to be attempted"—notably, British industry.[3] To set manufacturing industry in motion, therefore, he advocated protective tariffs, quotas, and bounties and at the same time encouraged the importation of advanced foreign technology by letting manufacturing materials enter duty free. In the short run, he recognized, manufactured goods would be provided to the citizens of America at high costs and prices. But over the longer run, he argued:

The contrary is the ultimate effect with every successful manufacture. When a domestic manufacture has attained to perfection, and has engaged in the prosecution of it a competent number of Persons, it invariably becomes cheaper. . . . The internal competition, which takes place, soon does away every thing like Monopoly, and by degrees reduces the price of the Article to the minimum of a reasonable profit on the Capital employed.[4]

Hamilton's message was carried forward and elaborated by Friedrich List (1841), whose magnum opus was published seven years after Germany began moving toward nation-statehood under the *Zollverein* (Customs Union). As might be expected of one who was imprisoned and then expelled from his native Württemberg for criticizing government bureaucracy and advocating the privatization of state enterprises, List carried a strain of paranoia into his writings. This shows up most strongly in his stinging criticisms of Adam Smith and the then accepted free trade views prevailing in England.

List examined the subsidies, import restraints, and other policy measures the English Crown had employed to encourage the growth of a strong manufacturing export industry. That England achieved its commercial eminence and power through free trade, he claimed, was "one of the greatest falsehoods promulgated in the present century."[5] It was a maxim adopted "to conceal the true policy of England under the . . . arguments which Adam Smith had discovered, in order to induce foreign nations not to imitate that policy."[6] A "new unprotected manufacturing power," he continued, "cannot possibly be raised up under free competition with a power which has long since grown in strength and is protected on its own territory."[7] Thus, like Hamilton, List advocated protection for "infant industries" until they were able to hold their own in world markets. Going beyond Hamilton, he emphasized the development of vocational education and the cultivation of science to help newly emerging German industry move to the industrial frontiers.

German economic development policy in fact hewed closely to Listian prescriptions. In the United States, the policies followed during most of the 19th century were a complex blend of Hamiltonian and Smithian precepts, with considerable protection for key industries, but also with more laissez faire and less direct government stimulation of industry than Hamilton had advocated. It is worth emphasizing that only in the 20th century, when the United States had surpassed England in industrial power, did America embrace free trade policies (at first briefly and then somewhat more consistently in the decades following World War II). Germany, too, moved toward free trade only after it had become one of the world's leading industrial powers. It is perhaps even more significant that NITT arguments, mirroring in many ways the analyses of Hamilton and List, have gained adherence at a time when America's leadership position in world trade is strongly challenged.

2.3 What Creates Comparative Advantage?

Smith and his classicist followers were vague about what factors gave rise to a nation's comparative advantage. In Ricardo's extended illustration, England exported cloth and imported wine from Portugal. Consistent with the spirit of his times, he believed that English cloth makers secured comparative advantage through their superior machinery, while the Portuguese were presumably endowed with more favorable winegrowing sunshine. During the 1920s and 1930s, a different and more elaborately articulated theory gained the support of most Western economists. Its pioneers were Sweden's Eli Heckscher (1919) and Bertil Ohlin (1933).

The so-called Heckscher-Ohlin theorem assumes that some nations (especially the more advanced ones) possess an abundance of capital; others (notably those in the developing world) have abundant and therefore cheap labor. Comparative advantage emerges when capital-rich nations specialize in commodities that require capital-intensive production processes while developing nations emphasize labor-intensive products. Thus, comparative advantage is determined by so-called factor abundance in the Heckscher-Ohlin model.

2.4   The Leontief Paradox

Although it was recognized, especially in Ohlin's richly perceptive *Interregional and International Trade*, that other variables influenced trading patterns in the short run, a significant blow to the Heckscher-Ohlin view was struck in what became known as the "Leontief Paradox." In 1953, the Russian-born American economist Wassily Leontief attempted to test the Heckscher-Ohlin predictions empirically by using so-called input-output statistics whose compilation he pioneered. He expected to find that the United States, at the time the world's most capital-rich nation, would run trade surpluses in capital-intensive manufactured goods and deficits in labor-intensive goods. Instead, he found the opposite: Americans exported labor-intensive items most successfully. This is not the trading pattern one would expect using the Heckscher-Ohlin model.

Reconciliations of this paradoxical finding with the then accepted wisdom were soon forthcoming. What America really enjoyed in abundance, it was argued, was human capital. At the time, its workers were among the best educated in the world, and the labor-intensive goods in which its industries ran trade surpluses were preponderantly skill-intensive goods. However, work to explain the paradox did not stop there. The result was an outpouring of research that laid the foundation for NITT.

While most modern economists still believe that comparative advantage governs international trade flows, there is heated and growing debate over what forces underlie a nation's comparative advantage and how comparative advantage can be established. NITT suggests that a nation can significantly alter its comparative advantage and hence its world trading position. As determinants of comparative advantage, NITT stresses R&D and technology, product life cycles, economies of scale, and the strategies pursued by enterprises possessing oligopoly and monopoly market power. The ability to manipulate these levers, NITT advocates hold, allows nations to shape and amend their comparative advantage.

Notes

1. Adam Smith, *An Inquiry into the Nature and Causes of the Wealth of Nations* (1776) (New York, N.Y.: Modern Library, 1937), Book IV, Chapter 2.

2. Alexander Hamilton, *Report on the Subject of Manufactures* (1791), in *The Papers of Alexander Hamilton*, Vol. X, ed. Harold C. Syrett (New York, N.Y.: Columbia University Press, 1966), p. 291.

3. Ibid., p. 266.

4. Ibid., p. 286.

5. Friedrich List, *The National System of Political Economy* (1841), English translation by Sampson S. Lloyd (London: Longmans, Green, 1916), p. 20.

6. Ibid., p. 295.

7. Ibid., p. 117.

3. Features of the New International Trade Theory

It must be made clear that two distinct schools of thought emerged in the paradigm-reformulating activity that followed publication of the Leontief Paradox. Early work emphasized finding explanations, often based on careful examination of real-world evidence, for the trading pattern anomalies identified by Leontief and other scholars. The second wave, which claims proprietary rights to formulating a "new" international trade theory, took those explanations and cast them in rigorously mathematical form. Following a pattern set by David Ricardo, international trade theory has been one of the most abstractly logical and, eventually, mathematical branches of applied economics. Work by NITT proponents in the 1980s and early 1990s transformed post-Leontief inductive insights into deductive mathematical models. When one hears claims that "there's nothing new in the new international trade lore" or that NITT is merely old wine in a new bottle, the likely interpretation is that the substance is old, even though the structure and packaging are new. This study stresses the substance of the theory over its technical elaborations.

3.1   Technology and R&D

One important perceptual change came in 1967, when two articles demonstrated that U.S. manufacturing industries achieved positive trade balances most successfully when they invested heavily in research and development.[1] Later, more detailed statistical work showed that, except in the special cases of farm commodities and coal, positive U.S. trade balances were more closely associated with technological innovation than with capital, labor, skill, minerals, or other traditional Heckscher-Ohlin endowments.[2] Studies covering numerous industrialized nations yielded further support: the more R&D-intensive a particular national industry was, compared with counterpart nations abroad, the more that national industry tended to have exports exceeding imports.[3]

That superior technology had something to do with comparative advantage in international trade was not a completely new insight. David Ricardo stressed with characteristic terseness the advantages of English machinery. Friedrich List elaborated:

9

There scarcely exists a manufacturing business which has not relations to physics, mechanics, chemistry, mathematics or to the art of design, &c. No progress, no new discoveries and inventions, can be made in these sciences by which a hundred industries and processes could not be improved or altered. In the manufacturing State, therefore, sciences and the arts must necessarily become popular. The necessity for education . . . induces men of special talents to devote themselves to instruction and authorship.[4]

Alfred Marshall, the leading British economist at the start of the 20th century, acknowledged wistfully in 1907 that England might be losing its advantage to other nations:

In the eighteenth century . . . England had something approaching a monopoly of the new methods of manufacture; and each bale of her goods would be sold . . . in return for a vast amount of the produce of foreign countries. . . . But . . . her improvements have been followed, and latterly often anticipated, by America and Germany and other countries; and her special products have lost nearly all their monopoly value.[5]

What was new in the work that followed Leontief's discovery was the statistical evidence that even within particular nations and across the industries of diverse nations, trade balances were systematically correlated with the intensity of an industry's technological innovation efforts.

3.2   The Product Life Cycle

A parallel development was the product life cycle theory, most closely identified with Raymond Vernon (1966). At the time, the United States, like England before it, was acknowledged as the world leader in most fields of industrial technology. Vernon postulated that in the early stages of the product life cycle, technological innovation tended to occur first in large national markets whose inhabitants enjoyed superior real incomes—notably the United States. The new products created through path-breaking R&D efforts were soon exported to other parts of the world —hence the favorable U.S. trade balance in high technology merchandise. To hurdle tariff barriers and adapt products to special national needs, however, innovators soon extended their production to other affluent nations. This could be done through licensing or by establishing foreign subsidiaries in nations previously served through exporting—thus the emergence of foreign direct investment (FDI), which was becoming increasingly prominent at the time Vernon wrote. FDI led to, among other consequences, "intrafirm" trade—that is, one division of a multinational corporation ships products to divisions located in other nations. Recent U.S. data reveal that roughly one-third of American merchandise exports goes to affiliated divisions overseas. However, as a product's technology matures, other enterprises begin to offer their own versions, and eventually price competition intensifies. With pressure on their prices, the original producers search for ways to reduce their costs. This often entails locating the now mature production operations in developing countries that offer the classical Heckscher-Ohlin advantage of abundant labor and low wage costs. Meanwhile, further innovations lead to the start of a new product life cycle in the most industrialized nations.

Since the early articulation of the product life cycle theory, several modifications have been recognized. First, an increasing number of enterprises have come to view their markets as global rather than national. Their R&D efforts are therefore not constrained by home market size and prosperity, and so the favorable position of the United States as the largest, richest national market has declined in importance as a determinant of where innovation occurs. The perfection of the European Union (EU) has had a similar effect in reducing U.S.-based firms' advantages. Second, the progression from early to mature stages of the product life cycle has accelerated as business firms throughout the world have become adept at imitating and improving new technology. Third, nations such as Japan and the Asian tigers, once favored only for their low wage costs in late stages of the product life cycle, have strengthened their technological capabilities so that their companies can play a pioneering role in the early stages. The upshot of these changes is that international competition for comparative advantage in high technology product trade has become more widely dispersed and fiercer than it once was.[6]

3.3 Intra-Industry Trade

Another important development has been the recognition that intra-industry trade is widespread. This new insight was precipitated in part by observation of the European Common Market's early history. When the Common Market, which became the European Community (EC) and recently the European Union, was created, most economists accepted the traditional Heckscher-Ohlin perspectives, anticipating that strong patterns of industrial specialization would emerge. For example, it was believed that Germany would specialize in exporting automobiles and electrical equipment; Italy, in exporting labor-intensive textiles and vegetables; and France, in exporting wine and haute couture. What actually happened was quite different.[7] German auto manufacturers exported the Mercedeses and Volkswagens that had first appealed to local tastes but that found a following elsewhere; French firms exported downscale Renaults and Citroen 2 CVs; and Italians exported tiny Fiats and powerful Ferraris. French winemakers exported their Bordeaux; Germans, their Moselles; and Italians, their Chiantis. Italian firms exported high-density polyethylene, while German chemical makers exported filled nylon, polyacetal, and other engineering resins. Outside the European Union, Japanese firms sell dynamic random access memory (DRAM) chips to America, while U.S.-based Intel ships microprocessors to Japan. Boeing assembles jumbo 747s; Airbus, aerodynamically efficient wide-body twins; and Canadair, commuter jets. Specialization has emerged on particular product variants within industries, and those specialized, or differentiated, products pass one another at national borders as they are traded to satisfy diverse consumer tastes. Trade is intra-industry rather than across specializing industries.

3.4   Economies of Scale

Seeking to explain the growth of intra-industry trade, economists have focused on the diversity of tastes, which was already apparent to Adam Smith, and, much more important, on economies of scale. Economies of scale enter in three main ways. First, the research, development, and testing required to launch a new product entail an often large, "lumpy," front-end commitment of resources. Once it is sunk, pro-rated R&D cost per unit subsequently sold is lower the more units that are sold. Thus, unit costs fall with rising output volume. Second, when industries encompass a wide diversity of products, each product may be manufactured in only modest production volumes, and so traditional "static" economies of scale loom large. If only a few thousand special-design washing machines are sold each year, they will be made at high cost using job-shop methods. If hundreds of thousands can be sold (e.g., to a worldwide market), unit costs can be reduced by automating parts production and assembly lines. Third, in many product categories, especially when technological advances have been implemented, economies of "learning by doing" occur. The more experience an organization accumulates in producing some product design, the more it can fine-tune its processes, find the best ways of organizing the work, and build worker skills, all of which lead to lower unit costs.

These product-specific economies of scale mean that the company initiating the manufacture of a particular product design is likely to enjoy a cost advantage in making that variant, while others enjoy similar advantages with their own models. This in turn implies, at least until products become sufficiently mature to be supplied from low wage nations, that each company enjoys a natural monopoly in the production of its own special designs for an international market. The result is what economists call "monopolistic competition"—blending elements of monopoly (each firm enjoying the cost advantages of supplying its own product variant) with competition (each product coming into more or less close competition with other variants).

3.5   Oligopoly

If the product-specific economies of scale are steep and pervasive, there may be room in a broad product category for only a few suppliers, each offering its individually differentiated family of products. Then domestic and even transnational market structures will approximate what economists call oligopoly—literally from the Greek, "few sellers."

Oligopoly poses two special difficulties for economists and others investigating patterns of international trade. One is methodological. The traditional theories of international trade have been based on the assumption of more or less pure (or perfect) competition. Under pure competition, there are large numbers of sellers, each too small relative to the overall market to have a perceptible influence on the product's price or the fate of particular competing firms. The pure competitors are said to be "price takers," accepting the prices thrown at them by the impersonal forces of supply and demand rather than having the power to set those prices. Under price taking, mathematical methods can be used to deduce powerful, quite general conclusions about how the competitive process will turn out, both for individual firms and for the markets (possibly international) they serve. Oligopoly is different. With only a few sellers, each recognizes that it can have a significant impact on the overall market outcome and on the fortunes of contending rival firms. The oligopolists are interdependent, and they are acutely aware of it.

Oligopoly is the economist's analogue of the three-body problem in physics, but it is even more difficult because each of the bodies is an aware, self-aggrandizing, human organization. With oligopoly, Company A recognizes that its best strategy choice is #1 if Companies B, C, and D choose strategy #2; but if the rivals choose #3, then the best choice for Company A may be strategy #4. If Company A chooses #4, however, that may induce its rivals to change their choices to some strategy other than #3, and so on. Both behaviorally and mathematically, the situation is extremely complicated—much more so than anything encountered in traditional trade theories.

The new international trade theory has joined other branches of economics in applying the theory of games (pioneered by John von Neumann and Oskar

Morgenstern in 1944) to wade analytically through the dilemmas that oligopolistic trade rivalries pose. The effort has been enormously fruitful. Numerous papers have been published predicting the consequences of international rivalries under richly varied assumptions. The remaining problem is that given the appropriate assumptions, virtually anything can be—and has been—predicted. As NITT pioneer Paul Krugman observes:

> At this point . . . the central problem of international trade theory is how to go beyond the proliferation of models to some kind of new synthesis. Probably trade theory will never be as unified as it was a decade ago, but it would be desirable to see empirical work begin to narrow the range of things that we regard as plausible outcomes.[8]

The other, and more important, difficulty is that comparative advantage in oligopolistic trade depends on the strategies of individual firms regarding R&D, plant location, pricing, product promotion, and the like. In economic jargon, comparative advantage is *endogenous*—i.e., it is the result of rival international oligopolists' actions and reactions and not bestowed on them by a benign providence. It is not *exogenous* to the economic system, or determined outside it, as in more traditional views. To phrase the point still another way, comparative advantage is something that is fought for and won, not merely inherited passively.

Notes

1. William Gruber, Dileep Mehta, and Raymond Vernon, "The R&D Factor in International Trade," *Journal of Political Economy*, Vol. 75 (February 1967), pp. 20-37; and Donald B. Keesing, "The Impact of Research and Development on United States Trade," *Journal of Political Economy*, Vol. 75 (February 1967), pp. 38-48.

2. Leo Sveikauskas, "Science and Technology in United States Foreign Trade," *Economic Journal*, Vol. 93 (September 1983), pp. 542-554.

3. Giovanni Dosi, Keith Pavitt, and Luc Soete, *The Economics of Technological Change and International Trade* (London: Harvester Wheatsheaf, 1990).

4. Friedrich List, *The National System of Political Economy* (1841), English translation by Sampson S. Lloyd (London: Longmans, Green, 1916), p. 162.

5. Alfred Marshall, *Principles of Economics* (London: The Macmillan Press Ltd, 1920), p. 561. The first edition of Marshall's *Principles* appeared in 1890. He added the last sentence of this

quotation with the fifth (1907) edition—at almost precisely the date to which scholars attribute the onset of England's climacteric.

6. F.M. Scherer, *International High-Technology Competition* (Cambridge, Mass.: Harvard University Press, 1992).

7. Bela Balassa, "Tariff Reductions and Trade in Manufactures," *American Economic Review*, Vol. 56 (June 1966), pp. 466-473.

8. Paul R. Krugman, *Rethinking International Trade* (Cambridge, Mass.: MIT Press, 1990), p. 261.

4. The Role of Strategy

It is in the role of strategy that the new international trade theory has made its most provocative contributions. If comparative advantage depends on the strategy choices made by particular companies, national success in the international trading arena also hinges on those strategy choices. Public policymakers may conclude that securing comparative advantage is too important to be left to the field generals—that is, to company managers. If companies can pursue advantage-winning strategies, so can nations. The new theories attempt to illuminate how, and with what consequences, comparative advantage can be won.

For nations to adopt trade-influencing strategies is hardly new. Since time immemorial, nation-states have been choosing among free trade, restrictive mercantilist policies, and complex (e.g., Hamilton-List) variants. Nor is it new to single out particular industries for special treatment, such as protective tariffs or subsidies. In the past, however, at least in nations ostensibly committed to free trade, industry-specific interventions have usually been taken when national governments have rejected the free trade premise that resources are fully employed, fearing that protracted unemployment of labor and capital might follow increased imports. Further, the industries receiving protection have been those that have organized political support for doing something about their plight, not those expected to contribute in some special way to the attainment of broader national goals. Disproportionately, those that have received strategic support from their governments might be characterized as "sunset" industries rather than the "sunrise" industries favored in NITT analyses.

NITT proponents acknowledge these political realities. But they argue, inter alia, that several Asian nations have been able to use NITT strategies successfully to develop their economies and improve their standards of living.[1] Thus, they see their theories as a challenge to governments to overcome special interest politics and develop more effective national strategies.

4.1   "Optimal" Tariffs

Early in the 20th century, and with increasing precision in later decades, economists began identifying cases in which governments might intervene with strategies to fine-tune individual industry terms of trade—that is, the ratio of the prices at which products are exported relative to the prices at which imports enter. The result was the theory of the "optimal tariff."[2]

To illustrate the standard case, consider a product imported by purely competitive intermediaries from purely competitive exporters. Accept also the conventional (although not logically necessary) assumption that the supply curve for exports is upward sloping; that is, the more of the product the importing nation buys, the higher will be the price at which the product enters, all else being equal. Competitive buyers are powerless to combat this situation, but astute governments have more potent strategic options. A government can put itself in the position of a monopsonist—a single buyer with power to influence the price at which it buys. By levying the optimal import tariff, it can raise the price to domestic consumers, choke off demand, and reduce the price received by overseas suppliers. The overseas firms will lose from this intervention, selling less at lower net prices. Domestic consumers will also lose. But the government as tariff collector will gain, and if it sets its tariff optimally, its gain is likely to exceed the loss to consumers, so it can impose the tariff and improve consumers' lot relative to the preintervention situation by using its tariff revenues to reduce other taxes at home.

The optimal tariff strategy has been advocated by many U.S. energy analysts. There is evidence that the tighter world oil markets are, the higher prices the Organization of Petroleum Exporting Countries (OPEC) is able to sustain. By levying a substantial tax on petroleum imported into the United States, it is argued, domestic and world demand will be reduced, and therefore OPEC prices net of tariff will be lower, all else being equal. The proceeds of the tariff can be used to reimburse consumers for the higher energy prices they will have to pay. The proposal has failed to secure political support, in part because energy users are a strong lobby and many citizens doubt that the tariff proceeds would in fact be refunded through lower taxes.

An analogous argument can be made for export tariffs. If a domestic industry provides a significant portion of the global market supply, the more output it exports, the lower will be the prices its members receive. If the industry members can combine into a monopoly, they can restrict their export sales to the quantity that maximizes their collective profit. If the industry is competitively structured, the members may be unable to wield sufficient power to achieve this result. But government can do the job for them by levying an export tariff. Foreign buyers will lose as a result, as will domestic producers. But if the tariff is set optimally, the government's tariff revenue gain can be more than enough to compensate producers for their lower net-of-tariff prices and output volume.

The Canadian government's imposition (under pressure from the United States) of a 15 percent export tariff on softwood lumber exports beginning in 1987 is believed to have been consistent with an optimal export tariff strategy from Canada's perspective.[3] U.S. timber owners gained; U.S. consumers lost. Canadian timber owners (mainly the provinces) and lumber operators also lost, but the Canadian government's revenue gain was more than enough to compensate the Canadian losers. Despite its attractions, the tariff strategy was abandoned in 1991, apparently because of administrative complexities and because it was difficult, given the wide differences in lumber industry conditions across provinces, to compensate the affected parties for their actual losses.[4]

Export tariffs are rare. But quite similar results can be achieved by organizing domestic firms into an export cartel. Then the firms themselves, rather than the government, capture the revenues realized by raising prices to foreign consumers. In a noteworthy exception to the free trading spirit embodied in GATT, nearly every industrialized nation exempts export cartels from domestic competition policy prohibitions against price fixing and other restrictive practices.[5] Attempts by importing nations to use their domestic competition laws to combat the high prices charged by export cartels pose complex legal questions. In a precedent-setting case, the European Community's Court of Justice held in 1988 that non-EC wood pulp exporters, including a group of U.S. firms claiming legal exemption under America's Webb-Pomerene export association law, violated EC law by selling in the Community at coordinated prices.[6]

Of course, when governments play such tariff and cartel games in an attempt to improve their own terms of trade and capture what amounts to monopoly or monopsony profits at the expense of their trading partners, the losing governments are tempted to retaliate. If Nation Y imposes restrictive import tariffs and Nation X responds by levying countervailing export tariffs or import tariffs on products purchased from Nation Y, Nation Y's net gains are likely to be transformed into losses, and almost everyone (except particularly strong or clever special interests) will be worse off. It was largely to curb the negative consequences of tariff wars that rules of the game were agreed to under GATT. This point will be discussed below.

4.2   Targeting

In addition to using tariffs and cartels to distort the terms of trade, nations (and their corporate champions) pursued strategies aimed at enhancing their comparative advantage long before NITT existed. The logic underlying these policies anticipated modern NITT models. During the 17th and 18th centuries, for

example, it was recognized that scientific work encouraged by the Royal Society
could benefit England's mercantile trading interests by improving sailing ships'
hydrodynamic design, cultivating stronger timbers, and facilitating more precise
navigation.[7]

It is well known that the Japanese government has pursued industrial policies
that seek to improve the technological capabilities of Japanese business firms.
Less well known is what a close call the choice of policies was and how
presciently the new international trade theories were anticipated. During the late
1940s, a heated debate took place within the Japanese government over industrial development strategies. Economists at the Japanese central bank argued
that, by the logic of the Heckscher-Ohlin theorem, Japan should take advantage
of its abundant low wage labor and emphasize the production of labor-intensive
products such as textiles and ceramics. Ministry of Trade and Industry (MITI)
representatives argued in reply that if this strategy were chosen, Japan would
remain an underdeveloped nation. Only by striving to embrace new, advanced
technologies in which Japan had no immediate comparative advantage, they
insisted, could Japanese industry develop and join the ranks of the leading
industrialized nations. The technology-forcing strategy was chosen, and the rest
is history.

A significant portion of the NITT literature recognizes that technological
pioneers enjoy "first mover" advantages such as strong patent portfolios,
consumer recognition and loyalty, "lock-in" effects resulting from having set
product standards, and enhanced ability to deter potential rivals intimidated by
early sunk investments.[8] Government interventions, it has been shown, can
bolster these first-mover advantages.

4.3   Retaliation

Most attempts, old and new, to apply strategic theory to international trade seek
an advantage over trading partners or foreign rivals. But trading partners and
rivals do not enjoy being bested, so they deploy countervailing strategies, which
often entail some form of retaliation.[9]

Game theory can help illuminate the various forms of retaliation in classic
tariff wars. The payoffs for two trading partners have a fairly typical structure
known to game theorists as a "Prisoner's Dilemma" matrix. To illustrate, there
are two strategies for Nation A (whose strategies are the rows of the matrix) and
Nation B (whose strategies are the columns): to impose a tariff on some class
of goods, or not to impose a tariff. The total net benefits to Nation A (profits for
producers, tariff revenue for governments, consumers' surplus for consumers)

are displayed as entries in the matrix:

		Nation B's Strategy Choices	
		NO TARIFF	TARIFF
Nation A's	NO TARIFF	100	0
Strategy			
Choices	TARIFF	150	50

Nation B's payoffs are symmetric. For example, just as A's payoff is 0 when A has no tariff and B has a tariff (as shown above), B's payoff is 0 when B has no tariff and A has a tariff.

In game theory parlance, imposing a tariff is a "dominant" strategy for each of the nations. This is so because, for example, having a tariff yields higher net benefits for Nation A whether Nation B has no tariff (A's gain is 150) or has a tariff (A's gain is 50). But this leads to a solution (each having tariffs) that provides net benefits (50 for each nation) inferior to those (100,100) that the nations could enjoy if *neither* imposed tariffs. Unencumbered trade is a positive-sum, win-win game in which most parties come out ahead. Trade with one-sided interventions leaves winners and losers, but the losers have strong incentives to retaliate. Retaliatory tariff wars are negative-sum games. Nations set multilateral rules of the game (e.g., GATT) and engage in bilateral negotiations to help avoid inferior, noncooperative solutions like the mutual tariff case.

International relationships analyzed under the new international trade theory often have different and more complex payoff structures. In particular, if there are compelling static or dynamic economies of scale, the total net payoffs summed across all parties involved may be greater with asymmetric outcomes (one firm dominates the sale of a product) than with symmetric outcomes (the market is shared equally). To illustrate, consider the rivalry of two firms with different national home bases in developing and marketing an integrated circuit. Each chooses between an aggressive learning curve pricing strategy, in which prices are kept well below current average costs, and a cost-based strategy, in which an attempt is made to keep prices above production costs once volume production has begun. The following payoff matrix shows only Firm A's results:

		Firm B's Strategy Choices	
		AGGRESSIVE	COST-BASED
Firm A's	AGGRESSIVE	−100	+300
Strategy			
Choices	COST-BASED	− 50	+ 10

If both firms pursue aggressive strategies, they fight a price war entailing large losses and end up sharing the market, with unit costs (because each has sacrificed the last possible cumulative doubling of output) higher than they might be. If both choose cost-based strategies, each earns positive profits, but again, the market is shared and the potential for achieving maximum scale economies is lost. If A fights a price war and B succumbs, B will suffer substantial losses while A dominates the market, attaining maximum scale economies and charging high prices (because of B's weak presence) during intermediate product life cycle stages.

In this example, there is no dominant solution, but one firm is likely to go for the large payoffs from an aggressive strategy, and the other firm may scurry to its national government for subsidies to permit an aggressive counterstrategy. In that case, large negative payoffs are experienced by both sides. The highest *combination* of payoffs ($300 - 50 = 250$) is associated with the asymmetric case. It may also be best for consumers.[10] If a nation were unwilling to let a single national champion dominate the entire industry, it could try to work out rules of the game that allowed Firm A to dominate the production of one type of integrated circuit and Firm B to dominate the production of another type, with intra-industry trade taking place to satisfy the market's diverse requirements. But achieving cooperation under circumstances like those depicted here is difficult, to say the least.

Although the real world of international high technology rivalry is much more complex than such game-theoretic illustrations convey, the scenarios presented above imply many possibilities beyond simple free trade stories. For example, in the DRAM "wars" of the mid 1980s, Japanese suppliers priced their 256-kilobit chips aggressively, probably incurring losses and inducing U.S. companies to appeal for government help.[11] After intergovernment negotiations, Japan agreed in July 1986 to have its chip makers charge prices not lower than their average costs in the preceding quarter (i.e., to abandon aggressive learning curve pricing) on all export sales. No such restraint was imposed on domestic sales. This should have raised the price of Japanese DRAMs to U.S. and European computer assemblers and other chip users, putting them at a disadvantage relative to their Japanese rivals. The firms that would have been disadvantaged were infuriated. The agreement should have helped U.S. DRAM producers, but most had fallen so far behind on their own learning curves that they dropped out of the market anyway, leaving the United States with only two domestic market suppliers.

However, the Japanese DRAM producers "chiseled" on the agreement, selling chips domestically to intermediaries who smuggled them to Hong Kong and then to America. The United States retaliated by placing prohibitive tariffs on Japanese laptop computers, small color television sets, and other electronic goods. Japan responded by having MITI directly control domestic suppliers' DRAM output. DRAM export prices again rose and remained high, hurting non-Japanese computer makers and consumers. MITI's production quotas triggered a chip shortage, discomfiting computer makers attempting to satisfy booming demand during 1987 and 1988. As new and higher powered DRAMs entered the market, one of the most complex episodes in the history of strategic trading rivalry came to an end.

The central point of these examples is that nations must consider the consequences of retaliation. Further, unilateral strategizing is rare. More often, numerous players participate in the game, deploying many different strategies, and players alter their strategies in reaction to the moves of one (or several) other players. Tit-for-tat retaliation becomes more difficult, and some winners may emerge. But the losers will find their own means of retaliating, and in the end, Hobbesian beggar-thy-neighbor strategizing is likely to lead to reduced payoffs in the world trading game.

Notes

1. Bruce R. Scott and George C. Lodge, *U.S. Competitiveness in the World Economy* (Boston, Mass.: Harvard Business School Press, 1985).

2. Nicholas Kaldor, "A Note on Tariffs and the Terms of Trade," *Economica*, Vol. 7 (November 1940), pp. 377-380; and Tibor Scitovsky, "A Reconsideration of the Theory of Tariffs," *Review of Economic Studies*, Vol. 9 (Summer 1942), pp. 89-110.

3. Joseph P. Kalt, "The Political Economy of Protectionism: Tariffs and Retaliation in the Timber Industry," in *Trade Policy Issues and Empirical Analysis*, ed. Robert E. Baldwin (Chicago, Ill.: University of Chicago Press, 1988), pp. 339-368.

4. See, for example, "Quebec to Rebate Part of Export Tax to Lumber Firms," *The Globe and Mail*, July 3, 1987, p. B1; "Softwood Pact Has Knotholes," *The Globe and Mail*, July 13, 1987, p. B1; and "Canada Ending Tax on Lumber," *The New York Times*, September 4, 1991, p. D1.

5. The proposed Havana Charter of 1947, which formed the basis for GATT, would have given a newly created International Trade Organization nonbinding powers to combat cartels affecting international trade. The charter was not ratified, in large measure because of U.S. reticence, and so the less sweeping GATT was adopted in its place. See F.M. Scherer, *Competition Policies for an Integrated World Economy* (Washington, D.C.: Brookings Institution, 1994).

6. *Åhström Osakeyhitö et al. v. Commission*, 1988 European Court Reports 5193 (1988).

7. Robert K. Merton, "Science and Economy of Seventeenth-Century England," in *The Sociology of Science*, ed. Bernard Barber and Walter Hirsch (Glencoe, Ill.: Free Press, 1962), pp. 67-88.

8. Gene M. Grossman and Elhanan Helpman, *Innovation and Growth in the Global Economy* (Cambridge, Mass.: MIT Press, 1992), Chapter 10.

9. See, for example, James A. Brander, "Rationale for Strategic Trade and Industrial Policy," and Gene M. Grossman, "Strategic Export Promotion: A Critique," in *Strategic Trade Policy and the New International Economics*, ed. Paul R. Krugman (Cambridge, Mass.: MIT Press, 1986), pp. 23-46, and pp. 47-68.

10. David R. Ross, "Learning to Dominate," *Journal of Industrial Economics*, Vol. 34 (June 1986), pp. 337-353.

11. Andrew R. Dick, "Learning by Doing and Dumping in the Semiconductor Industry," *Journal of Law & Economics*, Vol. 34 (April 1991), pp. 133-160; and Kenneth Flamm, *Mismanaged Trade: Strategic Trade and the Semiconductor Industry* (Washington, D.C.: Brookings Institution, forthcoming 1994).

5. Trade-Enhancing National Strategies

Despite objections to NITT, among other things for soft-pedaling retaliatory possibilities, its spread has rekindled age-old interest in activist trade policies. Nations can tap a vast menu of strategies to enhance the export competitiveness of their industries. This chapter provides examples of and evaluates the most important alternatives. The strategies are presented in roughly descending order of industry specificity. That is, policies narrowly targeted toward improving the export potential of individual industries or products are listed first, followed by more broadly based policies that affect a cluster of industries or a national economy.

5.1 Commodity Export Subsidies

Specific government subsidies to encourage the export of particular commodities have a lengthy history. They were provided by the British Crown to stimulate exports of naval stores and indigo from colonial America. They were assigned a prominent role in Alexander Hamilton's 1791 *Report on the Subject of Manufactures*, whose goal was to foster industrialization of the newly independent United States.[1] Government subsidies contravene principles accepted in GATT, but since agricultural commodities were exempted prior to the December 1993 Uruguay Round agreement, significant contemporary examples can be found.

The most important agricultural case is the subsidy system of the European Union's Common Agricultural Policy. Prices of basic grains such as wheat are supported within the Common Market at levels that encourage the accumulation of surpluses, but that are too high to permit exportation. When surplus products are exported, therefore, the European Union pays an export subsidy equal to the difference between the high internal price and the lower world price. Such subsidies have been one of the heaviest drains on EU budgets.

Retaliating against European policies, the U.S. Congress enacted in 1985 an Export Enhancement Program that grants subsidies, either in-kind from government stocks or (when stocks are low) in cash, permitting U.S. cereal grain exporters to match other nations' subsidized prices in world markets. Figure 1 shows trends over time in EC and U.S. wheat subsidies from 1987 to 1991. When world prices were high, the subsidies were modest; when they were low,

Figure 1
U.S. and EC Wheat Export Subsidies, 1987-91

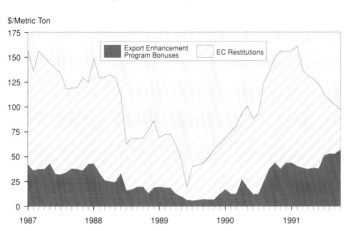

$/Metric Ton

Note: The EC Restitutions cover the entire graph.

Source: *Wheat Situation and Outlook* (Commodity Economics Division, Economic Research Service, U.S. Department of Agriculture, November 1991), WS 295.

the subsidies rose, for example, to a high of $150 per metric ton for European wheat in early 1991, when wheat was selling FOB New Orleans at roughly $120 per ton. During the 1990-91 crop season, EC wheat exports totaled 20 million metric tons, implying export subsidies of approximately $2.5 billion on wheat alone.

Such subsidies, combined with high domestic support prices, distort international crop cultivation patterns, injure nations such as Australia, Argentina, and Canada that are unable to retaliate, and burden taxpayers in the subsidizing nations. Reducing these subsidies was a major accomplishment of the Uruguay Round. Nations that export farm goods will decrease the volume of their subsidized exports by roughly 21 percent over six years, with most of the cutbacks taking place only in the sixth year. Bans on rice imports in Japan and South Korea will be replaced by high but declining tariffs. Quotas for imports of sugar, dairy products, and peanuts into the United States will be phased out and replaced by tariffs. Thus, the Uruguay Round made progress, but activist government policies remain a basic feature of much world trade in agricultural products.

5.2   Export Financing

Under a less extreme but narrowly targeted subsidy strategy, exporters are granted low cost government loans, often with provisions insuring losses against default by overseas customers. The United States Export-Import Bank (Ex-Im) was established in 1934 to help U.S. exporters match the financing terms available to competitors overseas. It provided net new credits averaging $1.5 billion per year during the 1960s and the 1970s, which declined to $0.8 billion per year between 1985 and 1989. Its longer-term loans were extended at rates approximately 2 percent below prevailing market rates in 1966[2] and 2.85 percent below its own borrowing cost in 1980.[3]

A leading beneficiary during the 1970s was the Boeing Company, causing wags to nickname Ex-Im "the Boeing Bank." Ex-Im's loans to Boeing were intended in part to counter the generous financing made available to Europe's Airbus Industrie. Escalation of this competitive financing struggle led the United States and Europe to agree in 1981 on minimum interest rates and maximum loan terms for aircraft export sales—an agreement formalized by the Organization for Economic Cooperation and Development (OECD) in 1985.[4]

In addition to export loan subsidies and even more generous subsidies on early production (to be discussed below), Airbus partner Messerschmitt-Boelkow-Blohm received subsidies (amounting to $2.47 million per aircraft sold in 1990) from the German government covering losses attributable to adverse currency fluctuations.[5] U.S. Trade Representative Carla Hills complained publicly that these were "the most reprehensible type of subsidy. . . . Once you subsidize currency fluctuations you're destroying the balance wheel that makes the trade mechanism work."[6] Following a U.S. petition to GATT, the program was abandoned prospectively (but not retroactively) in July 1992.

5.3   Government Favors Tied to Export Performance

The industrial development of Japan following World War II and of South Korea after the Korean War truce was marked by more subtle trade-oriented government subsidy policies. Both nations faced severe shortages of key raw materials and advanced industrial equipment. To finance their importation (along with licensed technological know-how) and hence to support industrialization, these nations felt compelled to increase their exports. This was done in part through a quid pro quo between government and business firms: the government allocated foreign currencies and low cost credit to selected companies, conditional on promises by the firms to achieve agreed-upon export targets.[7] The strategy was generally successful; both exports and the productivity of domestic manufacturers grew rapidly.

These programs were not uniquely responsible for the various Asian industrial "miracles," but they certainly contributed. One is hesitant to criticize previously poor nations for building their industrial capabilities, despite the short-run trade-distorting efforts their subsidies and exchange allocation efforts might have had. However, the programs were successful in part because at the early stages of their development, the countries were relatively small actors on the world trading stage, and the inroads their imports made were initially tolerated, even if not always welcomed, by large target-market nations. As Japanese and Korean exports grew, tensions mounted and countermeasures were enforced with increasing frequency. If analogous strategies were pursued by developing nations as large as China or India, it is likely that they would be resented and counteracted more quickly. The efforts of former Soviet bloc nations to earn hard currency by exporting steel, aluminum, and other materials to the West have encountered similar resistance.

5.4   Learning Curve Pricing

In many fields of technological innovation, one of the most important advantages a first mover has is the ability to race down learning curves and achieve low unit production costs before its latecomer rivals. This happens as operatives become more skilled at complex assembly tasks and engineers master the technical parameters needed to achieve high product yields. An innovating firm may enlarge its learning-by-doing lead not only by being the first to progress down the learning curve, but also by pricing aggressively (i.e., well below current average costs) to stimulate demand, build volume, and discourage rivals from following suit, as discussed in Chapter 4. Through a sufficiently aggressive policy, early movers can win protected monopoly positions during intermediate phases of the product life cycle.

In aircraft assembly, for instance, many analyses have revealed that learning curves have a slope of approximately 80 percent, which means that each doubling and redoubling of cumulative production leads to additional unit cost reductions of roughly 20 percent. Figure 2 shows a typical 80 percent learning curve for a jet airliner model. It is linear on doubly logarithmic coordinates. Producing the first unit costs about $260 million, and the tenth unit, $120 million. Unit costs fall to $60 million at 100 units, $46 million at 200 units, and $34 million at 500 units. If prices are held constant (except for inflation adjustments) at about $60 million per aircraft during most of the production

---

Figure 2

**An Example of an 80 Percent Learning Curve
for Jetliner Production**

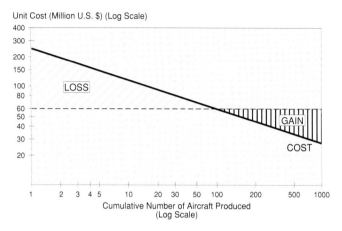

Source: Authors' example.

---

cycle, as is common, the manufacturer accumulates losses indicated by the diagonal area in Figure 2. By the time the 100th unit rolls off the assembly line, losses have mounted to $2.37 billion. Additional sales yield a price exceeding production cost, and the manufacturer achieves cumulative breakeven when 292 units have been completed. If further sales materialize (which is far from assured), they are highly profitable: e.g., total program profits mount to $2.25 billion at 400 units delivered, $4.66 billion at 500 units, and $7.3 billion at 600 units. Playing this "sporty game"[8] is less risky if a paternal government provides production subsidies in the early learning curve stages.[9] With a U.S. complaint to GATT over Airbus subventions pending, the EC authorities and the United States agreed in July 1992 that from then on, production and marketing subsidies would be avoided in civilian aircraft programs.

Similar price-volume relationships have been observed in the semiconductor industry, except that prices, starting from a level substantially below unit production costs at early stages in the production cycle, tend to fall over time (less rapidly than costs), rather than remaining steady. Again, breakeven and then profitability are achieved if a sufficiently large cumulative volume can be attained. Texas Instruments was one of the first practitioners of aggressive learning curve pricing outside the aviation field.[10] However, other U.S. and especially Japanese enterprises began embracing similar strategies, triggering bitter price wars in pocket calculators, early personal computer models, and integrated circuits. After sustaining substantial losses, Texas Instruments tried to back off from the strategy in the early 1980s, but Japanese integrated circuit manufacturers continued to pursue aggressive learning curve pricing. This led to the major international trade dispute described in Chapter 4.

There is only meager systematic evidence on the variables that influence companies' willingness to adopt aggressive learning curve pricing strategies. Japanese semiconductor manufacturers are said to have been able to play the game during the 1980s in part because they were affiliated with, and cross-subsidized by, *keiretsu* partners assembling computers, video recorders, and other semiconductor-using electronic apparatus.[11] American semiconductor makers claimed to be at a disadvantage because they lacked such vertically linked affiliates. However, there is an aircraft industry parallel. Lockheed and McDonnell-Douglas avoided bankruptcy owing to massive losses on their L-1011 and DC-10 wide-body airliner programs partly through cross-subsidies from their more profitable military divisions.

Because the gains from a learning curve pricing strategy are deferred until near the end of the product cycle, the strategy is more profitable the lower the cost of capital. Until the late 1980s, when capital flows abroad were decontrolled, Japanese companies enjoyed much lower capital costs than their American counterparts. The public policies that sustained earlier interest rate differentials contributed toward the difference in Japanese, compared to American, semiconductor makers' willingness to engage in aggressive pricing.

5.5   Advantages from a Protected Home Market

Achieving a high volume of production reduces unit costs whenever there are economies of scale—e.g., as a result of learning-by-doing, large front-end R&D investments, or the need for high volume production facilities or long production runs. A subtle form of government intervention can facilitate the realization of scale economies. The firm whose home market is reserved for domestic suppliers through trade barriers can gain an advantage over rivals whose home markets are open.[12] The firm—and its peers—can win all the sales in its home market plus a share of foreign market sales commensurate with the quality, date of availability, and price of its products. All else being equal, the enterprise with a sizable protected home market can achieve higher volume and hence (given scale economies) lower unit costs, and therefore can price more aggressively than rivals whose home market is open.

Nations strive to give their local producers this kind of scale economies advantage in diverse ways. One of the oldest methods is protection of the domestic market through high tariffs, quotas, and the exclusion of onshore investment by foreign multinational corporations. This attempt fails, however, if retaliatory tariffs and quotas deny access of the local champions to overseas markets. More subtle strategies are therefore pursued.

Attempts by would-be importers to hurdle tariff and quota barriers by building production facilities within the target market are hindered by general restrictions on foreign direct investment and by requirements that foreign plants achieve high "domestic content" targets. Domestic content restrictions will be discouraged under the Uruguay Round agreement, although the precise scope of the new rules remains uncertain.

Governments also foster, by law or informal suasion, "buy-at-home" policies on the part of procurement entities. The alleged closure of the Japanese market to many kinds of integrated circuits, fiber optic cables, computers, CT scanners, and metalworking machinery has been at the root of perhaps the most nettlesome trade rule disputes between the United States and Japan. For consumer goods, Japanese laws discouraging the construction of supermarkets large enough to carry both domestic and foreign products helped local manufacturers defend their production volume from the competition of would-be importers. The desire to eliminate trade-distorting national preferences in the procurement of telephone and analogous equipment has been a significant component of the European Union's 1992 "single market" initiative.

A related strategy is for governments to set technical standards that, at least initially, only local suppliers are prepared to meet. France's adoption of the SECAM color television standard and Germany's choice of PAL after the United States approved the National Television Standards Committee (NTSC) standard in 1953 is an important historical example. According to Laura Tyson, European nations adopted the multiplexed analog components (MAC) standard for high definition television (HDTV) broadcasting in 1986 so that "by having to go into a technology they didn't invent . . . the Japanese won't be able to test it on their home market."[13] The effort was abandoned, however, when European companies realized that the standard had been rendered obsolete by American work on digital HDTV systems.[14] Dissimilar standards with respect to automobile safety equipment and pollution control devices also give local manufacturers an advantage, as does the reluctance of national pharmaceutical regulatory agencies to accept data from foreign clinical tests.[15]

There may be good reasons for special national technical standards beyond the simple desire to maintain a protected market for local champions. Without a compelling rationale, however, buy-at-home mandates divide up world markets into small fiefdoms, prevent the full realization of cost-reducing scale economies, and inhibit the responsiveness of producers to variegated consumer tastes within national markets.

5.6 Coercive Market-Opening Measures

Trading nations have reacted to the closure of significant national markets with a variety of market-opening measures. The arrival of Commodore Perry's "black ships" in Japan during 1853 was a dramatic early demonstration of U.S. aspirations. A more current example is the "Super 301" clause written into U.S. trade law in 1988.[16] Under it, the U.S. Trade Representative was directed to identify nations whose markets were unfairly closed to U.S. exports or which in other ways (e.g., by granting only weak patent protection) were considered to be sustaining unfair trade practices. Market-opening negotiations were then to be initiated, and if they were not successful within 18 months, punitive retaliatory tariffs on the target nations' exports to the United States were to be threatened.

This threat led Japan in 1989 and 1990 to cooperate in a "Structural Impediments Initiative" seeking to alter numerous subtle import-discouraging practices. Even before the Super 301 weapon existed, Japanese trade authorities agreed in 1986, as part of a dumping case settlement, to help American manufacturers raise their share of semiconductor sales in the Japanese home market from 8 percent in 1986 to 20 percent in 1991.

If successful, such unilateral market-opening initiatives foster the expansion of international trade, with all its concomitant benefits. But they also engender resentment and hostility, increasing the likelihood of brinkmanship and miscalculation, which in turn can lead to the breakdown of trading relationships. In the long run, they are apt to do more harm than good. Multilateral negotiations and, if need be, sanctions imposed by impartial authorities such as GATT dispute resolution committees and the World Court, appear preferable as a means of prying markets open.

5.7 Cartel Formation and Dumping

Dumping is conventionally defined as the sale of goods in foreign markets at prices (net of freight) lower than those charged in the home market. One reason dumping may be attractive is that prices have been elevated in the home market through monopolistic restrictions, freeing up capacity that can be used profitably by selling at lower prices abroad. There is reason to believe that systematic dumping was practiced by the U.S. steel and petroleum industries around the turn of the century. A prominent recent case was the Japanese sale of television sets in the U.S. market during the 1960s and 1970s, provoking legal battles eventually resolved by the U.S. Supreme Court.[17] Many facts remain in dispute, but it is clear that Japanese television manufacturers maintained a cartel that held domestic prices at relatively high levels and that an export cartel (created with the explicit encouragement of MITI) failed to keep prices to U.S. outlets above "check price" points, below which antidumping reactions were feared. By 1976, the Japanese share of U.S. color television sales had risen abruptly to 36 percent, and U.S. television set producers began exiting from the industry.

There are plausible reasons why a national government might tolerate domestic market cartels, burdening its consumer constituents with high prices while foreigners are served more cheaply. For one, dumping usually enhances total output, making it possible to realize economies of scale more fully. Second (but inconsistent with the facts of the television receiver case), cartels may be authorized to protect domestic firms from temporary recession-induced financial crises. Third, governments may adopt a dynamic (e.g., "Schumpeterian") view of cartels, seeing them, and the dumping they encourage, as a means of building up industry profits, to be reinvested in technological advances and plant expansion. A facilitating condition probably applicable in Japan is that producers and consumers are seen as intersecting groups. Consumers pay high cartel prices, but as workers they also receive wages higher than would otherwise prevail.

Even though target-nation consumers often benefit from the low prices quoted by price-discriminating foreign firms, dumping has long been viewed as an unfair practice that distorts trade and undermines the profitability (and, in extreme cases, the continued existence) of target-nation manufacturers. However, controversy persists over how dumping should be identified in legal proceedings.[18] Particularly nettlesome problems arise in connection with products such as aircraft and semiconductors, which are subject to strong learning-by-doing effects. If prices are not set below average cost in the early learning curve stages, when costs are particularly high, new products may fail to capture sales from incumbents, and the low cost segments of the learning curve may never be reached. Also, when costs fall with cumulative experience, the incremental cost of an additional unit produced is substantially lower because of the learning effect than the current full cost of that unit. Antidumping rules that focus on full costs rather than on incremental costs, as is standard practice in both the United States and the European Union, can prevent pricing that sustains desirable learning by doing. How dumping is defined in such cases, and also under worldwide recession conditions (e.g., in the steel industry during the early 1990s), deserves to be reevaluated in an appropriate international forum.

5.8   Coordination of Industry Investments

A more unusual government practice is the coordination of industry investments to ensure that scale economies are achieved to the maximum possible extent without creating excess capacity. The Japanese steel industry during the 1960s and early 1970s provides the clearest example.[19] The industry was expanding rapidly, in part through exporting. To realize the lowest possible cost per ton of steel produced, new blast furnaces, oxygen converter shops, and primary rolling mills had to be built with annual capacities of 3 to 4 million ingot tons, or about one-third the annual growth of Japanese steel production. If all companies expanded their plants in large-scale lumps simultaneously, excess capacity was likely to result. But if, fearing this, the companies expanded in smaller increments or failed to invest at all, their equipment would be of inefficiently small scale, and Japan's progress toward becoming cost competitive in world markets might be jeopardized. To secure the most favorable tradeoff between scale economies and capacity utilization, MITI regimented a new blast furnace construction rotation program, letting each company have its turn at planned intervals. Compliance with the program was enforced by rationing access to restricted foreign currency reserves (e.g., to purchase iron ore and coal). MITI's hold on steel makers waned after Japan became a full (Article 8) member of the International Monetary Fund in 1964 and gradually relaxed foreign exchange controls.

Maximum efficiency was pursued through a somewhat different coordination strategy in the Japanese ball and roller bearing industry.[20] In bearings, the key to low costs is attaining long production runs. With MITI's encouragement, the Japanese bearing manufacturers divided up assignments so that only a single company produced any specific low- or medium-volume design. In 1969, the British government responded to this development and the aggressive export campaign it facilitated by brokering a merger of three leading U.K. bearing manufacturers to form a new firm, RHP Ltd. Product line rationalization measures were undertaken within RHP.

33

Government coordination efforts have also been mounted with respect to industries plagued by chronic excess capacity. Japan's MITI orchestrated capacity-shedding cartels in aluminum, shipbuilding, and several other industries during the 1970s, as did the European Union's industrial directorate for the synthetic fibers industry. The results were not uniformly efficiency enhancing, for in some cases political pressures made it necessary to reduce capacity by the same proportion in efficient firms as in high cost producers, ensuring the survival of more small-scale, high cost capacity than what probably would have resulted under the pressure of competition.[21]

One is reluctant to fault governmentally coordinated efforts to raise industrial productive efficiency. However, when cartelized coordination of capacity expansion (or reduction) is accompanied by the elevation of home market prices and the systematic dumping of output overseas, the objections raised in the "Cartel Formation and Dumping" section reappear.

5.9   Provision of Cheap Raw Materials

Particularly vexing issues surface when national governments provide, from natural resource endowments, raw materials to local industries at what appear to be bargain prices. Several Middle Eastern nations have vast reserves of petroleum whose incremental production cost is a few dollars per barrel—well below world market prices. They also have natural gas that, if not utilized, may have to be flared or reinjected into wells at high cost. To an increasing extent, they have been transferring those resources at below-market prices to domestic petrochemical manufacturing complexes, conferring on the favored operations a substantial cost advantage vis à vis foreign rivals. Similarly, although the facts have been vigorously disputed, U.S. logging and sawmill interests accused the Canadian provincial governments during the 1980s of providing timber to sawmills at below-market prices, allegedly enhancing softwood lumber and shingle exports to the United States and as a result undermining the prices received by U.S. lumber operators.

When raw materials are provided to "downstream" domestic industries at prices below their free market values, production of the downstream industries may be stimulated artificially at the expense of efficient operators elsewhere. However, determining the correct free market price of such resources is often difficult. If, for instance, the next-best use of by-product natural gas from Persian Gulf oil wells is flaring or expensive liquefaction and transportation to overseas markets, local utilization as a petrochemical feedstock can be economically rational. Then the price at which the resource is transferred downstream becomes a matter of secondary importance. Similarly, the opportunity cost of bulky, hard-to-transport timber from remote Canadian forests may be quite low, as Adam Smith recognized two centuries ago:

> Barren timber for building is of great value in a populous and well-cultivated country, and the land which produces it affords a considerable rent. But in many parts of North America the landlord would be much obliged to any body who would carry away the greater part of his large trees.[22]

Three rounds of the Canadian softwood lumber dispute aroused unusually acute tensions.[23] In the third round, a binational panel convened under procedures of the U.S.-Canada Free Trade Agreement rejected the U.S. government's claim that countervailable subsidies had in fact been provided.[24] Similar problems are likely to recur as oil-producing nations seek to expand their natural resource-using industries. A principled resolution of the issues is essential.

5.10   Subsidizing Research and Development

Recognizing the key role that technological innovation plays in modern theories of comparative advantage, governments have sought, and economists have refined, strategies to enhance the technological capabilities of domestic industries and to increase the likelihood that leadership positions in key technologies are captured. Through subsidies and tax rebates, facilitating technologies can be cultivated, specific development projects can be accelerated, and the flow of well-educated talent from the schools to industry can be stimulated.

Trade among industrialized nations has come to depend to an increasing degree on offering technologically superior new products and using superior production processes.[25] National governments strive to enhance their domestic firms' comparative advantage by subsidizing research and development programs. These interventions range widely in the degree to which they advance specific commercial objectives. At one extreme is the subsidization of basic scientific research, the results of which may facilitate applied work in narrowly defined industries or across a broad spectrum of industries at home and abroad. Somewhat more specific is what has come to be called "precompetitive generic research," i.e., on concepts and materials so broadly applicable and susceptible to diffusion that no single firm can secure a likely competitive advantage over its peers from having done the work.[26] A variant is the development of production processes and other infrastructure technology that will be available to, and used by, virtually all members of an industry. Examples include the silicon refining techniques and semiconductor fabricating equipment developed under the Japanese Very Large Scale Integration (VLSI) Project during the 1970s and the analogous effort of Sematech in the United States since 1987.

Still more specific are government contracts to develop for military or other public purposes equipment that can be put to dual use in the defense and civilian sectors. Boeing's ticket of admission to eventual leadership in the jetliner industry, the B-707, embodied structural concepts perfected through the B-47 bomber program. Boeing's progress down its 707 learning curve was accelerated by parallel production of the nearly identical KC-135 tanker for the U.S. Air Force. General Electric and Westinghouse, leaders in the now dormant U.S. civilian nuclear reactor industry, built on experience accumulated in the U.S. Navy's nuclear propulsion reactor program.

The public exchequer may also support or subsidize R&D on products destined expressly or primarily for civilian markets. Examples include the various Airbus jetliners, the Concorde and the U.S. supersonic transport (SST) aircraft (the latter abandoned after subsidized development outlays approached $1 billion), high definition television in Europe,[27] one-megabit DRAM integrated circuits in Korea, and pharmaceuticals such as AZT and Ceredase in the United States. Finally, all varieties of commercially oriented R&D are stimulated through special tax privileges, e.g., when tax credits are granted on expenditures, or increases in the expenditures, for R&D in Canada, Sweden, Germany, and (since 1981) the United States.[28]

The desirability of government financial support probably varies inversely with the industry specificity of the subject research or development efforts. There is widespread consensus that too little basic scientific research would be performed were it not for generous public funding. The rationale for support of precompetitive generic research is analogous. There is more disagreement on whether, or to what extent, public funds should be channeled toward the development of products that will be sold mainly in commercial markets. Because comparative advantage depends to an increasing degree on technological innovation rather than natural endowments of labor and capital, hefty development subsidies to national champions distort international trading patterns. However, it is difficult to retreat from a practice when "everybody does it." A step toward control of a particularly egregious case was taken in 1992 with the U.S.-EC agreement on airliner subsidies. One facet of the agreement limits direct development subsidies to 33 percent of R&D outlays and requires repayment on a royalty per plane basis. The agreement also caps indirect subsidies, such as identifiable benefits derived from parallel military aircraft developments, at 4 percent of total company sales.

The Uruguay Round treaty contains broader guidelines for such subsidies. It limits government subsidies in technology-intensive industries to 50 percent of applied research outlays (defined as work up to first prototypes) and 75 percent on basic research.

5.11 Intellectual Property Protection

Especially for high technology products and easily copied items such as videotapes and computer software, trading patterns can be altered by the choices that nations make toward granting or withholding intellectual property rights, e.g., in the form of patents, copyrights, and trademarks. Patent protection for pharmaceuticals has been particularly contentious. As of 1989, drug products were not patentable under the national laws of nearly half the 101 signatories to the Paris Convention for the Protection of Intellectual Property. Between 1969 and 1987, Canada granted drug product patents, but required patent holders to license their patents at quite modest royalties (typically 3 percent of the licensee's sales) to generic drug providers. When patent protection is weak or nonexistent, the new products of research-oriented pharmaceutical firms often face tough price competition from local imitators. Also, vigorous drug product exporting industries have emerged in some nations that confer no product patent rights—e.g., in Italy until 1978 and India more recently. Drugs are shipped from there to other nations with weak patent protection, competing with the products of the innovative research-oriented companies.

The U.S. government has aggressively used its Section 301 law to induce recalcitrant nations to strengthen their intellectual property laws. Pressed by strong industry lobbies, the United States joined with Japan and the European Union to accord high priority in Uruguay Round negotiations to securing greater uniformity of intellectual property laws among GATT signatories. Most but not all of the nations with weak laws are developing countries. Historically, nations have tended to maintain weak intellectual property institutions at the stage in their economic development when they are absorbing technology much more rapidly from abroad than they generate it locally. When developing countries undertake few innovations locally and when, as is also common, they possess severely limited reserves of the "hard" currencies with which royalties and multinational corporation profits are repatriated, they are likely to oppose strenuously demands that they strengthen their patent and copyright laws. Few international trade questions have juxtaposed interests conflicting more sharply than the bilateral and multilateral negotiations over intellectual property.

The Uruguay Round agreement embodies a compromise. Signatories will extend their intellectual property laws to provide 20 years of protection from the time of application for inventions and as much as 50 years for computer software. But developing countries will be given at least 5 years to phase in its provisions for most inventions, and for pharmaceutical patents, a 10-year phase-in period. Whether the agreement will be accepted by all developing countries, who participated only marginally in the final negotiations, remains uncertain.

5.12   Subsidizing Worker Education

The level and breadth of workers' skills have a crucial impact on the kinds of industries in which nations can be internationally competitive. Skills in turn are honed through educational programs.[29] Much government-supported education is so general that advantages derived from it by specific industries are difficult to trace. However, there are exceptions. Germany's great success in exporting complex mechanical products is often attributed to its extensive occupation-specific vocational training programs for the two-thirds of its young citizens who do not pursue a university education track. The German state and federal governments contribute an estimated $10 billion per year to apprenticeship and vocational training programs implemented jointly with business firms.[30]

U.S. Secretary of Labor Robert B. Reich has placed high priority on expanding analogous programs in the United States.[31] Despite the lack of thorough-going government-supported apprenticeship programs in the United States, special cases can be identified. The highly successful U.S. pharmaceutical companies, for example, hire many R&D scientists only after they have earned their Ph.D.s under government scholarships and received post-doctoral training at the National Institutes of Health. Japan targets the state-supported university training of its engineers and scientists by periodically announcing "visions" as to which industries are expected to grow rapidly and hence demand high technology talent.[32] Few objections have been raised to the government support of these and other educational programs, including those that are narrowly targeted and those that are not.

5.13   Trade-Influencing Macroeconomic Policies

International trade flows are influenced by a host of policies that operate mainly at the macroeconomic level. These include monetary policies that affect exchange rates, such as the attempt of Japan to hold the yen at values favorable to exports during the 1960s and the similar policy of Turkey in recent years. They also include tax structure choices. Most industrialized nations rely heavily on value added taxes, which under GATT rules can be remitted on export sales. By emphasizing income taxes and shunning the value added tax alternative, the United States has put itself at an international trading disadvantage (compensated to an unknown degree by exchange rate adjustments).

The monetary and fiscal policies of nations often conflict, creating inter alia international trade tensions like those experienced in Europe in 1992 and 1993 owing to high German interest rates. Such policy conflicts can hardly be avoided. The Group of Seven and similar consultative groups have attempted to smooth out the differences, but with only limited success.

5.14   Enforcement

Finally, all too often international trade is influenced by bribery, collusion, and political payoffs. Some nations have laws outlawing these practices, while others do not. Even if two nations have similar laws on the books, they may be enforced quite differently. As a member of the British-North American Committee commented: "I have frequently found that our foreign competitors who may have similar laws in their own countries are not held accountable for their conduct overseas."

Laws in these areas and the degree of enforcement can be a major parameter of trade policy. Several U.S. and European corporations have formed a group called "Transparency International" whose purpose is to recommend ways to attack this problem.

Notes

1. Hamilton observes: "But the greatest obstacle of all [toward developing manufacturing industry] consists . . . in the bounties, premiums and other aids which are granted . . . by the nations, in which the establishments to be imitated are previously introduced." Alexander Hamilton, *Report on the Subject of Manufactures* (1791), in *The Papers of Alexander Hamilton*, Vol. X, ed. Harold C. Syrett (New York, N.Y.: Columbia University Press, 1966), p. 268.

2. Robert E. Baldwin, *Nontariff Distortion of International Trade* (Washington, D.C.: Brookings Institution, 1970), p. 53.

3. Jordan Jay Hillman, "The Export-Import Bank of the United States," in *Government Agencies*, ed. Donald R. Whitnah (Westport, Conn.: Greenwood Press, 1983), p. 199.

4. Laura D. Tyson, *Who's Bashing Whom? Trade Conflict in High-Technology Industries* (Washington, D.C.: Institute for International Economics, 1992), p. 175.

5. Monopolkommission, 1990/1991 Report, *Wettbewerbspolitik oder Industriepolitik* (Baden-Baden: Nomos, 1992), p. 390.

6. Tyson, *Who's Bashing Whom?* p. 206.

7. Takatoshi Ito, *The Japanese Economy* (Cambridge, Mass.: MIT Press, 1992), pp. 67-69 and 114-119; and Alice H. Amsden, *Asia's Next Giant: South Korea and Late Industrialization* (Oxford: Oxford University Press, 1989), pp. 72-78.

8. John Newhouse, *The Sporty Game* (New York, N.Y.: Knopf, 1982).

9. Robert E. Baldwin and Paul R. Krugman, "Industrial Policy and International Competition in Wide-Bodied Jet Aircraft," in *Trade Policy Issues and Empirical Analysis*, ed. Robert E. Baldwin (Chicago, Ill.: University of Chicago Press, 1988), pp. 45-78; and Gernot Klepper, "Entry into the Market for Large Transport Aircraft," *European Economic Review* (June 1990), pp. 775-803.

10. "Selling Business a Theory of Economics," *Business Week*, September 8, 1973, pp. 85-90.

11. Ito, *The Japanese Economy*, pp. 192-195; and Tyson, *Who's Bashing Whom?* pp. 100-101.

12. Paul R. Krugman, *Rethinking International Trade* (Cambridge, Mass.: MIT Press, 1990), Chapters 12 and 13.

13. Tyson, *Who's Bashing Whom?* p. 241.

14. Richard Stevenson, "Europe Gives Up Its Advanced-TV Project," *The New York Times*, February 20, 1993, p. 46.

15. On Japan's drug test policy, see Tyson, *Who's Bashing Whom?* p. 60. On the U.S. insistence on domestic tests, see U.S. Office of Technology Assessment, *Pharmaceutical R&D: Costs, Risks, and Rewards* (Washington, D.C.: U.S. Government Printing Office, 1993), pp. 153-154.

16. Jagdish Bhagwati and Hugh T. Patrick, eds., *Aggressive Unilateralism* (Ann Arbor, Mich.: University of Michigan Press, 1990).

17. *Matsushita Electric Industrial Co. Ltd. et al. v. Zenith Radio Corp. et al.*, 475 U.S. 574 (1986). See also David Schwartzman, *The Japanese Television Cartel* (Ann Arbor, Mich.: University of Michigan Press, 1993).

18. Richard Boltuck and Robert E. Litan, eds., *Down in the Dumps: Administration of the Unfair Trade Laws* (Washington, D.C.: Brookings Institution, 1991).

19. Kiyoshi Kawahito, *The Japanese Steel Industry* (New York, N.Y.: Praeger, 1972), pp. 22-48; and Thomas K. McCraw and Patricia O'Brien, "Production and Distribution," in *America vs. Japan*, ed. Thomas K. McCraw (Boston, Mass.: Harvard Business School Press, 1986), pp. 92-100.

20. F.M. Scherer et al., *The Economics of Multi-Plant Operation: An International Comparisons Study* (Cambridge, Mass.: Harvard University Press, 1975), pp. 313-314.

21. Compare R.W. Shaw and S.A. Shaw, "Excess Capacity and Rationalisation in the West European Synthetic Fibres Industry," *Journal of Industrial Economics* (December 1983), pp. 149-166; Joseph L. Bower, *When Markets Quake: The Management Challenge of Restructuring Industry* (Boston, Mass.: Harvard Business School Press, 1986); and M.J. Peck, Richard Levin, and Akira Goto, "Picking Losers: Public Policy Toward Declining Industries in Japan," in *Government Policy Towards Industry in the United States and Japan*, ed. John B. Shoven (Cambridge: Cambridge University Press, 1988), pp. 193-239.

22. Adam Smith, *An Inquiry into the Nature and Causes of the Wealth of Nations* (1776) (New York, N.Y.: Modern Library, 1937), Book I, Chapter 11.

23. See the discussion of the export tariff imposed as a result of the second round settlement, p. 18 supra.

24. *In the Matter of Certain Softwood Lumber Products,* Article 1904 Binational Panel Review, U.S.-Canada Free Trade Agreement, Decision of the Panel, May 6, 1993.

25. See, for example, F.M. Scherer, *International High-Technology Competition* (Cambridge, Mass.: Harvard University Press, 1990).

26. See, for example, U.S. Office of Science and Technology Policy, Executive Office of the President, *U.S. Technology Policy* (Washington, D.C., September 26, 1990); and United Kingdom, Chancellor of the Duchy of Lancaster, *Realising Our Potential: A Strategy for Science, Engineering, and Technology* (London: HMSO, May 1993).

27. Tyson, *Who's Bashing Whom?* p. 239, reports expenditures by national European governments on HDTV of at least $250 million as of 1989. In 1993, when the project was canceled, further government contributions of $600 million were planned.

28. Joseph J. Cordes, "Tax Incentives and R&D Spending: A Review of the Evidence," *Research Policy*, 1989, pp. 119-133; and Bronwyn H. Hall, *R&D Tax Policy During the Eighties: Success or Failure?* National Bureau of Economic Research Working Paper, November 1992.

29. Frederick W. Crawford and Simon Webley, *Continuing Education and Training of the Workforce* (London: British-North American Committee, 1992).

30. Stephen Kinzer, "Germans' Apprentice System Is Seen as Key to Long Boom," *The New York Times*, February 6, 1993, pp. A1 and A5.

31. Robert B. Reich, *The Work of Nations* (New York, N.Y.: Knopf, 1991), Chapters 20 and 21.

32. Daniel Okimoto, *Between MITI and the Market* (Stanford, Calif.: Stanford University Press, 1989), p. 17.

6.   Policy Implications and Future Prospects

Nations can use a vast array of strategies to alter their comparative advantage and increase their export competitiveness. Many of these strategies are not new. This study has presented examples dating back to the time of Adam Smith and Alexander Hamilton. What is new is that the NITT model accords more intellectual support and credence to certain trade-enhancing strategies. Also, technological advances have increased the ability of government decision-makers to embrace trade-enhancing strategies.

The trade-enhancing strategies reviewed in Chapter 5 were presented in roughly descending order of industry specificity. One way to evaluate them might be to draw general dividing lines within the group of arrayed policies. The most narrowly targeted policies might be rejected as causing more harm than good. More broadly based policies (such as intellectual property protection, human resource policies, and general macroeconomic measures) might be seen to do more good than harm. However, it is difficult to avoid scrutinizing policies in individual strategy areas. For example, some macroeconomic policies may enhance a nation's international competitiveness and at the same time benefit the world economy, while others (such as distortions of foreign exchange rates) could increase one nation's exports at the expense of rival nations.

6.1   Different NITT Schools

To progress further, it must be recognized that there are many shades of NITT. In considering the policy implications, it is useful to divide NITT into two groups.

Hard-core, or hyperactive, NITT deemphasizes the problems caused by retaliation. It assumes either that meaningful retaliation will not take place or that new, more sophisticated strategies can be devised to counter other nations' retaliation. It also minimizes the political difficulties experienced in fine-tuning comparative advantage and distinguishing between industries that will receive strategic support and those that will not. Thus, hard-core NITT asks: never mind comparative advantage as it exists today; where can comparative advantage be won in the future? Also, are there specific industries that seem to have large growth potential or that will facilitate further developments in new areas? Are there high value added fields or high technology industries in which advantage can be captured?

Hard-core NITT would advocate policies that move a nation and its corporations into these favored fields. Such policies could include industry targeting, export subsidies, product development subsidies, measures to reduce the cost of capital and other inputs, blocking market access to secure economies of scale, human resource policies favorable to specific industries' growth, and a wide range of government-private sector partnerships geared toward favored industries. Carried to an extreme, hard-core NITT would treat international trade as a kind of economic warfare.

At the other end of the spectrum is cautious NITT. It recognizes that retaliation is a serious problem. It also acknowledges that although comparative advantage can in principle be altered, fine-tuning is difficult to do well in politicized environments. Instead of favoring specific sectors or industries, cautious NITT would have policymakers become more sensitive to the climate in which business enterprises function. For example, macroeconomic policies in general, and tax policies specifically, should encourage R&D and rapid technological development. Cautious NITT would also consider the implications for international trade of many other policies that traditionally have been implemented only with a domestic perspective. For example, education and training, infrastructure investment, and fiscal policy would be seen to have a significant impact on comparative advantage.

Hard-core NITT would place less emphasis on multilateral trade agreements and more on bilateral or regional deals. While cautious NITT would not give up on multilateralism, it too would argue for intensified interest in bilaterialism and regional trading blocs.

Hard-core NITT insists that trade-enhancing national strategies have important consequences. Other nations use those strategies; therefore, we must also enhance our export competitiveness. In other words, it accepts the logic of the Prisoner's Dilemma as essentially inescapable. A more cautious response would be as follows: NITT demonstrates the importance and pervasive influence of trade-enhancing national strategies. It also shows the significance of nontariff trade barriers. Thus, it points to the need for more international rules of the road covering not only trade per se, but also cross-border investment, subsidies to activities preceding production for export, intellectual property rights, tax policies, other domestic policies that influence trade, and the conduct of multinational enterprises.

6.2   GATT and Super GATT

Since the end of World War II, the main thrust of multilateral trade negotiations has been to lower tariff barriers.[1] Much progress has been made. With tariff rates on most commodities at relatively low levels, at least in the 117 nations subscribing to GATT, the vast array of nontariff barriers and trade-distorting strategies commands center stage.

This means that the agenda of multilateral and regional trade talks will have to continue to move successfully beyond tariff issues. The history of GATT negotiations, especially since the Uruguay Round began in 1986, shows how difficult it is to adopt new rules of the road on nontraditional trade issues. Although the Uruguay Round made some progress on nontariff barriers and the extension of its rules beyond trade in manufactured goods and minerals, it left many vexing questions unresolved. In fact, it could be argued that the Uruguay Round agreement was reached only because tough nontariff barrier issues were swept under the rug. Nevertheless, NITT—and the possibility of escalating trade warfare—makes it urgent that progress be achieved on a wider array of issues.

This study has identified several imperatives that warrant high priority in post-Uruguay multilateral trade policy rounds.

• Economically rational definitions must be provided on what constitutes dumping when there is substantial learning by doing and when a recession induces industry participants to set prices below fully allocated unit costs.

• The progress that has been achieved in limiting agricultural and R&D subsidies must be extended.

• What comprises subsidy in the provision of government-owned natural resources must be defined with greater precision.

• There must be strenuous efforts to reduce nontariff barriers to trade such as buy-at-home preferences, the establishment of trade-distorting product quality standards, and the closure of distribution channels. Some of these problems may be best resolved in the context of broadly agreed-upon multilateral competition policy rules.

• Multilateral competition policy agreements should delimit the permissible operating bounds for cartels and other restrictive agreements with trade-distorting effects.

• National policies governing foreign direct investment must be harmonized.

• The coverage of multilateral trading rules to service and financial industries must be extended.

Not to be overlooked in future agenda-setting are some important questions that have not been the focus of this study, such as standards for avoiding environmental pollution by export-oriented industries and provisions governing the international mobility of workers.

The European Union, the United States, Canada, and Mexico have gone beyond GATT in shaping new rules of the road for regional trading blocs. The problem with regional trading blocs is their exclusionary character. Reform of the multilateral system under GATT would be a "first best" solution, while regional trading blocs remain a "second best" solution. Regional trading blocs instigate a "them versus us" mentality, whereas the GATT has been open to all who are willing to follow certain basic principles, such as most favored nation (MFN) treatment. Under MFN, tariff or other concessions offered to one trading partner must be extended to all.

If GATT cannot be reformed fast enough to embody new international rules covering nontariff trade barrier issues, there will be intense pressure on public and private sector decisionmakers to deploy NITT trade-enhancing strategies to an increasing extent. One solution to this dilemma might be to create a "Super GATT" for nations willing to progress beyond basic GATT principles. At one level, there would be a basic GATT centered on MFN and other widely accepted multilateral provisions. Nations accepting rules covering nontariff trade barrier issues would ratify Super GATT. Unlike a regional trading bloc—which is exclusionary and not open to all nations—the Super GATT would be open to any nation agreeing to follow its mandates.[2]

The world community faces a limited window of opportunity to formulate new rules of the international trading game. If this window of opportunity is not seized, then the trade-enhancing strategies crystallized under NITT could spread well beyond their current bounds. Once this happens, it will be difficult to get the genie back into the bottle.

6.3   Future Prospects

New economic theories often promise much more than they can deliver. The promised gains from NITT-supported policies may prove to be illusionary.

Nevertheless, the new ways of looking at international trade are exerting a significant influence on public and private sector decisionmakers. Many NITT insights have real merit. Global trading patterns are far more complex than classical trade theory implies. In the end, NITT may not supplant the classical views. Instead, the two paradigms may coexist. International trade will be like the proverbial blind man touching the elephant: which view is best depends on which part of the elephant is being explored. In the long term, NITT—if combined with the standard model—could make the mainstream paradigm a far richer and much improved model of international trade.

The Uruguay Round achieved significant progress. But many unfinished tasks remain. The spread of NITT thinking makes it all the more urgent to formulate new rules concerning dumping, nontariff barriers, investments, the environment, and many forms of government subsidy and promotion. The hope of the authors is that from a better understanding of NITT will come a renewed sense of urgency concerning the implementation of new rules of the road, which in turn will limit the likelihood of future trade distortions and trade warfare.

Notes

1. Sir James Ball, *The Causes of Rising Protectionism* (London: British-North American Research Association, Occasional Paper No. 7, 1987).

2. Richard S. Belous, "Super GATT: A Way to Avoid Clashes Between GATT and Regional Trading Blocs," *Looking Ahead*, Vol. XV, No. 2 (July 1993), pp. 3-7.

References

Amsden, Alice H. *Asia's Next Giant: South Korea and Late Industrialization*. Oxford: Oxford University Press, 1989.

Balassa, Bela. "Tariff Reductions and Trade in Manufactures." *American Economic Review*, Vol. 56, June 1966.

Baldwin, Robert E., and Paul R. Krugman. "Industrial Policy and International Competition in Wide-Bodied Jet Aircraft." In *Trade Policy Issues and Empirical Analysis*, ed. Robert E. Baldwin. Chicago, Ill.: University of Chicago Press, 1988.

Baldwin, Robert E. *Nontariff Distortion of International Trade*. Washington, D.C.: Brookings Institution, 1970.

Ball, Sir James. *The Causes of Rising Protectionism*. London: British-North American Research Association, Occasional Paper No. 7, 1987.

Belous, Richard S. "Super GATT: A Way to Avoid Clashes Between GATT and Regional Trading Blocs." *Looking Ahead*, Vol XV, No. 2, July 1993.

———, ed. *Global Corporations and Nation-States: Do Companies or Countries Compete?* Washington, D.C.: National Planning Association, 1991.

Belous, Richard S., and Jonathan Lemco, eds. *NAFTA as a Model of Development: The Benefits and Costs of Merging High and Low Wage Areas*. Washington, D.C.: National Planning Association, 1993.

Bhagwati, Jagdish, and Hugh T. Patrick, eds. *Aggressive Unilateralism*. Ann Arbor, Mich.: University of Michigan Press, 1990.

Boltuck, Richard, and Robert E. Litan, eds. *Down in the Dumps: Administration of the Unfair Trade Laws*. Washington, D.C.: Brookings Institution, 1991.

Bower, Joseph L. *When Markets Quake: The Management Challenge of Restructuring Industry*. Boston, Mass.: Harvard Business School Press, 1986.

Brander, James A. "Rationale for Strategic Trade and Industrial Policy." In *Strategic Trade Policy and the New International Economics*, ed. Paul R. Krugman. Cambridge, Mass.: MIT Press, 1986.

Cordes, Joseph J. "Tax Incentives and R&D Spending: A Review of the Evidence." *Research Policy*, 1989.

Crawford, Frederick W., and Simon Webley. *Continuing Education and Training of the Workforce*. London: British-North American Committee, 1992.

Dick, Andrew R. "Learning by Doing and Dumping in the Semiconductor Industry." *Journal of Law & Economics*, Vol. 34, April 1991.

Dosi, Giovanni, Keith Pavitt, and Luc Soete. *The Economics of Technological Change and International Trade*. London: Harvester Wheatsheaf, 1990.

Flamm, Kenneth. *Mismanaged Trade: Strategic Trade and the Semiconductor Industry*. Washington, D.C.: Brookings Institution, forthcoming 1994.

Grossman, Gene M. "Strategic Export Promotion: A Critique." In *Strategic Trade Policy and the New International Economics*, ed. Paul R. Krugman. Cambridge, Mass.: MIT Press, 1986.

Grossman, Gene M., and Elhanan Helpman. *Innovation and Growth in the Global Economy*. Cambridge, Mass.: MIT Press, 1992.

47

References

Gruber, William, Dileep Mehta, and Raymond Vernon. "The R&D Factor in International Trade." *Journal of Political Economy*, Vol. 75, February 1967.

Hall, Bronwyn H. *R&D Tax Policy During the Eighties: Success or Failure?* National Bureau of Economic Research Working Paper, November 1992.

Hamilton, Alexander. *Report on the Subject of Manufactures* (1791). In *The Papers of Alexander Hamilton*, Vol. X, ed. Harold C. Syrett. New York, N.Y.: Columbia University Press, 1966.

Heckscher, Eli F. "The Effect of Foreign Trade on the Distribution of Income" (1919). Translated in American Economic Association. *Readings in the Theory of International Trade*. Philadelphia, Pa.: Blakiston, 1949.

Hillman, Jordan Jay. "The Export-Import Bank of the United States." In *Government Agencies*, ed. Donald R. Whitnah. Westport, Conn.: Greenwood Press, 1983.

Ito, Takatoshi. *The Japanese Economy*. Cambridge, Mass.: MIT Press, 1992.

Jackson, John H. *Restructuring the GATT System*. London: The Royal Institute of International Affairs, 1990.

Kaldor, Nicholas. "A Note on Tariffs and the Terms of Trade." *Economica*, Vol. 7, November 1940.

Kalt, Joseph P. "The Political Economy of Protectionism: Tariffs and Retaliation in the Timber Industry." In *Trade Policy Issues and Empirical Analysis*, ed. Robert E. Baldwin. Chicago, Ill.: University of Chicago Press, 1988.

Kawahito, Kiyoshi. *The Japanese Steel Industry*. New York, N.Y.: Praeger, 1972.

Keesing, Donald B. "The Impact of Research and Development on United States Trade." *Journal of Political Economy*, Vol. 75, February 1967.

Keynes, John Maynard. *The General Theory of Employment, Interest, and Money*. New York, N.Y.: Harcourt, Brace, and World, 1936.

Klepper, Gernot. "Entry into the Market for Large Transport Aircraft." *European Economic Review*, June 1990.

Krugman, Paul R. *Rethinking International Trade*. Cambridge, Mass.: MIT Press, 1990.

Leontief, Wassily. "Domestic Production and Foreign Trade: The American Capital Position Reconsidered." *Proceedings of the American Philosophical Society*, Vol. 97, September 1957.

List, Friedrich. *The National System of Political Economy* (1841). English translation by Sampson S. Lloyd. London: Longmans, Green, 1916.

Marshall, Alfred. *Principles of Economics*. London: The Macmillan Press Ltd., 1920.

McCraw, Thomas K., and Patricia O'Brien. "Production and Distribution." In *America vs. Japan*, ed. Thomas K. McCraw. Boston, Mass.: Harvard Business School Press, 1986.

Merton, Robert K. "Science and Economy of Seventeenth-Century England." In *The Sociology of Science*, ed. Bernard Barber and Walter Hirsch. Glencoe, Ill.: Free Press, 1962.

Monopolkommission. 1990/1991 Report. *Wettbewerbspolitik oder Industriepolitik*. Baden-Baden: Nomos, 1992.

Newhouse, John. *The Sporty Game*. New York, N.Y.: Knopf, 1982.

Ohlin, Bertil. *Interregional and International Trade.* Cambridge, Mass.: Harvard University Press, 1933.

Okimoto, Daniel. *Between MITI and the Market.* Stanford, Calif.: Stanford University Press, 1989.

Peck, M.J., Richard Levin, and Akira Goto. "Picking Losers: Public Policy Toward Declining Industries in Japan." In *Government Policy Towards Industry in the United States and Japan,* ed. John B. Shoven. Cambridge: Cambridge University Press, 1988.

Reich, Robert B. *The Work of Nations.* New York, N.Y.: Knopf, 1991.

Ricardo, David. *The Principles of Political Economy and Taxation* (1817). London: Penguin Books Ltd., 1971.

Ross, David R. "Learning to Dominate." *Journal of Industrial Economics,* Vol. 34, June 1986.

Scherer, F.M. *Competition Policies for an Integrated World Economy.* Washington, D.C.: Brookings Institution, 1994.

———. *International High-Technology Competition.* Cambridge, Mass.: Harvard University Press, 1992.

Scherer, F.M. et al. *The Economics of Multi-Plant Operation: An International Comparisons Study.* Cambridge, Mass.: Harvard University Press, 1975.

Schwartzman, David. *The Japanese Television Cartel.* Ann Arbor, Mich.: University of Michigan Press, 1993.

Scitovsky, Tibor. "A Reconsideration of the Theory of Tariffs." *Review of Economic Studies,* Vol. 9, Summer 1942.

Scott, Bruce R., and George C. Lodge. *U.S. Competitiveness in the World Economy.* Boston, Mass.: Harvard Business School Press, 1985.

Shaw, R.W., and S.A. Shaw. "Excess Capacity and Rationalisation in the West European Synthetic Fibres Industry." *Journal of Industrial Economics,* December 1983.

Smith, Adam. *An Inquiry into the Nature and Causes of the Wealth of Nations* (1776). New York, N.Y.: Modern Library, 1937.

Spencer, Barbara J. "What Should Trade Policy Target?" In *Strategic Trade Policy and the New International Economics,* ed. Paul Krugman. Cambridge, Mass.: MIT Press, 1986.

Sveikauskas, Leo. "Science and Technology in United States Foreign Trade." *Economic Journal,* Vol. 93, September 1983.

Tyson, Laura D. *Who's Bashing Whom? Trade Conflict in High-Technology Industries.* Washington, D.C.: Institute for International Economics, 1992.

United Kingdom, Chancellor of the Duchy of Lancaster. *Realising Our Potential: A Strategy for Science, Engineering, and Technology.* London: HMSO, May 1993.

U.S. Office of Science and Technology Policy, Executive Office of the President. *U.S. Technology Policy.* Washington, D.C., September 26, 1990.

U.S. Office of Technology Assessment. *Pharmaceutical R&D: Costs, Risks, and Rewards.* Washington, D.C., 1993.

Vernon, Raymond. "International Investment and International Trade in the Product Cycle." *Quarterly Journal of Economics,* Vol. 80, May 1966.

von Neumann, John, and Oskar Morgenstern. *Theory of Games and Economic Behavior.* Princeton, N.J.: Princeton University Press, 1944.

Members of the
British-North American Committee*

---

* Membership on the Committee does not necessarily signify agreement with all the contents of its publications.

Roger Bexon
Chairman
Laporte Plc
London

Carrol D. Bolen
Vice President
Director, Specialty Plant Products
Pioneer Hi-Bred International, Inc.
Des Moines, IA

William E. Bradford
President and Chief Operating Officer
Dresser Industries, Inc.
Dallas, TX

Richard C. Breeden
Former Chairman, Securities and
Exchange Commission
Chairman, Financial Services Group
Vice Chairman, International Financial
Services Group
Coopers & Lybrand
New York, NY

Roger H. Bricknell
Vice President
GE Industrial & Power Systems
General Electric Company
Schenectady, NY

Martin Broughton
Deputy Chairman and
Group Chief Executive
BAT Industries Plc
London

Tom Burlison
Deputy General Secretary
G.M.B.
London

Derek H. Burney
Chairman, President and Chief Executive
Officer
BCE Telecom International Inc.
Montreal, Quebec

Dominic Cadbury
Executive Chairman
Cadbury Schweppes Plc
London

Sir Peter Cazalet
Chairman
APV Plc
London

Samuel F. Chevalier
Vice Chairman
The Bank of New York
New York, NY

Richard M. Clarke
Chairman
Yankelovich Partners Inc.
Westport, CT

Sir Robert Clarke
Chairman
United Biscuits (Holdings) Plc
West Drayton, Middlesex

Sir Anthony Cleaver
Chairman
AEA Technology
London

John P. Coghlan
Executive Vice President/
Schwab Institutional
Charles Schwab & Co., Inc.
San Francisco, CA

Marshall A. Cohen
President and Chief Executive Officer
The Molson Companies Limited
Toronto, Ontario

Ralph H. Cooper
President, European Community Group
The Coca-Cola Company
Atlanta, GA

Albert J. Costello
Chairman and Chief Executive Officer
American Cyanamid Company
Wayne, NJ

Paul J. Hoenmans
Executive Vice President
Mobil Oil Corporation
Fairfax, VA

Sir Simon Hornby
Chairman
W.H. Smith Group Plc
London

Professor Hendrik S. Houthakker
Professor of Economics
Harvard University
Cambridge, MA

Roger Hurn
Chairman
Smiths Industries Plc
London

Paul H. Inderbitzin
Executive Vice President
America Re-Insurance Co.
Princeton, NJ

M.B. Ingle
President
Imcera Group, Inc.
Northbrook, IL

Donald P. Jacobs
Dean
J.L. Kellogg Graduate School
of Management
Northwestern University
Evanston, IL

John T. Joyce
President
International Union of
Bricklayers & Allied Craftsmen
Washington, DC

Thomas E. Kierans
President and Chief Executive Officer
C.D. Howe Institute
Toronto, Ontario

Sir John Kingman
Vice Chancellor
University of Bristol
Bristol, U.K.

Paul Kofmehl
Chairman
Franklin Health Group Inc.
Ramsey, NJ

Norman Lessels
Chairman
Standard Life
Edinburgh, Scotland

William A. Liffers
Vice Chairman (Retired)
American Cyanamid Company
Wayne, NJ

Sir Richard Lloyd
Deputy Chairman
Hill Samuel Bank Ltd.
London

Pierre Lortie
Chairman
Bombardier Capital Group
Montreal, Quebec

Hon. Malcolm R. Lovell, Jr.
President and Chief Executive Officer
National Planning Association
Washington, DC

Roger Lyons
General Secretary
MSF
London

Dr. Paul MacAvoy
Dean
Williams Brothers Professor
Management Studies
Yale School of Organization and
Management
New Haven, CT

53

Robert B. Peterson
Chairman and Chief Executive Officer
Imperial Oil Limited
Toronto, Ontario

Sir Antony Pilkington
Chairman
Pilkington, Plc
St. Helens, Merseyside

Brian Pitman
Chief Executive
Lloyds Bank Plc
London

George J. Poulin
General Vice President
International Association of Machinists
& Aerospace Workers
Stamford, CT

Alfred Powis
Chairman
Noranda Inc.
Toronto, Ontario

Ian Prosser
Chairman and Chief Executive
BASS Plc
London

Lee R. Raymond
Chairman and Chief Executive Officer
Exxon Corporation
Irving, TX

Sir Bob Reid
Chairman
British Railways Board
London

William R. Rhodes
Vice Chairman
Citibank, N.A.
New York, NY

Miles Rivett-Carnac
Chairman
Baring Asset Management Ltd.
London

Professor Ben Roberts
Professor Emeritus
Department of Industrial Relations
London School of Economics
London

Robert D. Rogers
President and Chief Executive Officer
Texas Industries, Inc.
Dallas, TX

Professor Harold B. Rose
Esmée Fairbairn Visiting Professor
of Finance
London Business School
London

James H. Ross
Chief Executive
Cable & Wireless Plc
London

Frank A. Rossi
Chairman
FAR Holdings Company
Chicago, IL

Patrick G. Ryan
President and Chief Executive Officer
Aon Corporation
Chicago, IL

Guy Saint-Pierre
President and Chief Executive Officer
SNC-LAVALIN GROUP Inc.
Montreal, Quebec

Frederic V. Salerno
Vice Chairman and President
Nynex-President World Wide Services
NYNEX Corporation
White Plains, NY

Thomas R. Saylor
Cambridge, England

Arthur R.A. Scace
Managing Partner
McCarthy Tetrault
Toronto, Ontario

Members of the BNAC

Derek Wanless
Director; Group Chief Executive
National Westminister Bank Plc
London

Viscount Weir
Chairman
The Weir Group Limited
Glasgow, Scotland

Alan Wheatley
Director
N M Rothschild & Sons Ltd
London

Frederick B. Whittemore
Advisory Director
Morgan Stanley and Company, Inc.
New York, NY

C.W. Wilson
President and Chief Executive Officer
Shell Canada Limited
Calgary, Alberta

L.R. Wilson
Chairman, President, and
Chief Executive Officer
BCE Inc.
Montreal, Quebec

Margaret S. Wilson
Chairman and Chief Executive Officer
Scarbroughs
Austin, TX

Humphrey Wood
Chairman
Vinten Group Plc
London

Stephen P. Yokich
Vice President and Director
UAW General Motors Department
International Union, UAW
Detroit, MI

Lord Younger of Prestwick
Chairman
Royal Bank of Scotland, Plc
Edinburgh, Scotland

Sponsoring Organizations

The British-North American Research Association was inaugurated in December 1969. Its primary purpose is to sponsor research on British-North American economic relations in association with the British-North American Committee. Publications of the British-North American Research Association as well as publications of the British-North American Committee are available from the Association's office, Grosvenor Gardens House, 35-37 Grosvenor Gardens, London SW1W 0BS (Tel. 071-828 6644). The Association is registered as a charity and is governed by a Council under the chairmanship of Sir David Plastow.

The National Planning Association is an independent, private, nonprofit, nonpolitical organization that carries on research and policy formulation in the public interest. NPA was founded during the Great Depression of the 1930s when conflicts among the major economic groups—business, labor, agriculture—threatened to paralyze national decisionmaking on the critical issues confronting American society. NPA is dedicated to the task of getting these diverse groups to work together to narrow areas of controversy and broaden areas of agreement as well as to map out specific programs for action in the best traditions of a functioning democracy. Such democratic and decentralized planning, NPA believes, involves the development of effective government and private policies and programs not only by official agencies but also through the independent initiative and cooperation of the main private sector groups concerned.

To this end, NPA brings together influential and knowledgeable leaders from business, labor, agriculture, and the applied and academic professions to serve on policy committees. These committees identify emerging problems confronting the nation at home and abroad and seek to develop and agree upon policies and programs for coping with them. The research and writing for these committees are provided by NPA's professional staff and, as required, by outside experts.

In addition, NPA's professional staff undertakes research through its central or "core" programs designed to provide data and ideas for policymakers and planners in government and the private sector. These activities include research on national goals and priorities, productivity and economic growth, welfare and dependency problems, employment and human resource needs, and technological change; analyses and forecasts of changing international realities and their implications for U.S. policies; and analyses of important new economic, social, and political realities confronting American society.

In developing its staff capabilities, NPA has increasingly emphasized two related qualifications. First is the interdisciplinary knowledge required to understand the complex nature of many real-life problems. Second is the ability to bridge the gap between theoretical or highly technical research and the practical needs of policymakers and planners in government and the private sector.

Malcolm R. Lovell, Jr., is President and Chief Executive Officer.

NPA publications, including those of the British-North American Committee, can be obtained from the Association's office, 1424 16th Street, N.W., Suite 700, Washington, D.C. 20036 (Tel. 202-884 7623).

The C.D. Howe Institute is an independent, nonpartisan, nonprofit research and education institution. It carries out and makes public independent analyses and critiques of economic policy issues and translates scholarly research into choices for action by governments and the private sector.

The Institute was established in 1973 by the merger of the C.D. Howe Memorial Foundation and the Private Planning Association of Canada (PPAC). The Foundation had been created in 1961 to memorialize the late Right Honorable C.D. Howe, who served Canada in many elected capacities between 1935 and 1957, including Minister of Trade and Commerce. The PPAC was a unique forum created in 1958 by leaders of business and labor for the purpose of carrying out research and educational activities on economic policy issues.

While its focus is national and international, the Institute recognizes that Canada is composed of regions, each of which may have a particular perspective on policy issues and different concepts of what should be national priorities.

A Board of Directors is responsible for the Institute's general direction and for safeguarding its independence. The President is the chief executive and is responsible for formulating and carrying out policy, directing research, and selecting staff. In order to promote the flexibility and relevance of its work, the Institute's high quality professional staff is intentionally kept small and is supplemented with a number of scholars and compatible institutions.

Participation in the Institute's activities is encouraged from business, organized labor, trade associations, and the professions. Through objective examinations of different points of view, the Institute seeks to increase public understanding of policy issues and to contribute to the public decisionmaking process.

Thomas E. Kierans is President and Treasurer.

The Institute's offices are located at: P.O. Box 1621, Calgary, Alberta T2P 2L7; and 125 Adelaide Street East, Toronto, Ontario M5C 1L7 (Tel. in Toronto, 416-865 1904).

Publications of the British-North American Committee

BN-39
The World Economy: Trends and Prospects for the Next Decade
A Special Report for the BNAC's 25th Anniversary in 1994
by Professor Sir James Ball, June 1994 (£10.00, U.S.$15.00)

BN-38
The Question of Saving
by Harold Rose, March 1991 (£4.00, U.S.$8.00)

BN-37
On Preserving Shared Values: A Committee Statement on the 40th Anniversary of the North Atlantic Treaty
May 1989 (£1.25, U.S.$2.00)

BN-36
The GATT Negotiations 1986-1990: Origins, Issues and Prospects
by Sidney Golt, November 1988 (£6.00, U.S.$10.00)

BN-35
Stiffening the Sinews of the Nations: Economic Infrastructure in the United States, United Kingdom, and Canada
by Simon Webley, December 1985 (£4.00, U.S.$6.00)

BN-34
The Process of Innovation
by Nuala Swords-Isherwood, October 1984 (£5.00, U.S.$8.00)

BN-33
Governments and Multinationals: Policies in the Developed Countries
by A.E. Safarian, December 1983 (£4.00, U.S.$8.00)

BN-32
Trade Issues in the Mid 1980s
by Sidney Golt, with a Committee Policy Statement, October 1982 (£3.50, U.S.$7.00)

BN-31
The Newly Industrializing Countries: Adjusting to Success
by Neil McMullen, November 1982 (£3.50, U.S.$7.00)

BN-30
Conflicts of National Laws with International Business Activity: Issues of Extraterritoriality
by A.H. Hermann, August 1982 (£3.00, U.S.$6.00)

BN-29
Industrial Innovation in the United Kingdom, Canada and the United States
by Kerry Schott, July 1981 (£2.25, U.S.$5.00)

BN-28
Flexible Exchange Rates and International Business
by John M. Blin, Stuart I. Greenbaum and Donald P. Jacobs, December 1981 (£3.00, U.S.$8.00)

Publications of the BNAC

BN-27
A Trade Union View of US Manpower Policy
by William W. Winpisinger, April 1980 (£1.75, U.S.$3.00)

BN-26
A Positive Approach to the International Economic Order, Part II: Non-Trade Issues
by Alasdair MacBean and V.N. Balasubramanyam, May 1980 (£2.25, U.S.$5.00)

BN-25
New Patterns of World Mineral Development
by Raymond F. Mikesell, September 1979 (£2.25, U.S.$5.00)

BN-24
Inflation Is a Social Malady
by Carl E. Beigie, March 1979 (£2.00, U.S.$4.00)

BN-23
A Positive Approach to the International Economic Order, Part I: Trade & Structural Adjustment
by Alasdair MacBean, October 1978 (£1.75, U.S.$3.00)

BN-22
The GATT Negotiations 1973-79: The Closing Stage
by Sidney Golt, with a Committee Policy Statement, May 1978 (£1.50, U.S.$3.00)

BN-21
Skilled Labour Supply Imbalances: The Canadian Experience
by William Dodge, November 1977 (£1.50, U.S.$3.00)

BN-20
The Soviet Impact on World Grain Trade
by D. Gale Johnson, May 1977 (£1.75, U.S.$3.00)

BN-19
Mineral Development in the Eighties: Prospects and Problems
A report prepared by a group of Committee members with a Statistical Annex by Sperry Lea, November 1976 (£1.50, U.S.$3.00)

BN-18
Skilled Labour Shortages in the United Kingdom: With Particular Reference to the Engineering Industry
by Gerry Eastwood, October 1976 (£1.50, U.S.$3.00)

BN-17
Higher Oil Prices: Worldwide Financial Implications
A Policy Statement by the British-North American Committee and a Research Report by Sperry Lea, October 1975 (£1.50, U.S.$3.00)

BN-16
Completing the GATT: Toward New International Rules to Govern Export Controls
by C. Fred Bergsten, October 1974 (80p, U.S.$2.00)

BN-15
Foreign Direct Investment in the United States: Opportunities and Impediments
by Simon Webley, September 1974 (80p, U.S.$2.00)

BN-14
The GATT Negotiations, 1973-75: A Guide to the Issues
by Sidney Golt, April 1974 (£1.00, U.S.$2.00)

BN-13
Problems of Economic Development in the Caribbean
by David Powell, compiled from a study by Irene Hawkins, November 1973 (80p, U.S.$2.00)

BN-12
The European Approach to Worker-Management Relationships
by Innis Macbeath, October 1973 (£1.00, U.S.$2.50)

BN-11
An International Grain Reserve Policy
by Timothy Josling, July 1973 (40p, U.S.$1.00)

BN-10
Man and His Environment
by Harry G. Johnson, August 1973 (40p, U.S.$1.00)

BN-9
Prospective Changes in the World Trade and Monetary System: A Comment
A Statement by the BNAC, October 1972 (30p, U.S.$0.75)

BN-8
Multinational Corporations in Developed Countries: A Review of Recent Research and Policy Thinking
by Sperry Lea and Simon Webley, March 1973 (80p, U.S.$2.00)

BN-7
Sterling, European Monetary Unification, and the International Monetary System
by Richard N. Cooper, March 1972 (40p, U.S.$1.00)

BN-6
Multinational Corporations and British Labour: A Review of Attitudes and Responses
by John Gennard, January 1972 (80p, U.S.$2.00)

Issues Paper-3
Unfinished Tasks: The New International Trade Theory and the Post-Uruguay Round Challenges
by F.M. Scherer and Richard S. Belous, May 1994 (£6.00, U.S.$9.00)

Issues Paper-2
The Changing World of Finance and Its Problems
by Harold Rose, March 1993 (£6.00, U.S.$9.00)

Issues Paper-1
Continuing Education and Training of the Workforce
by Frederick W. Crawford and Simon Webley, November 1992 (£9.00, U.S.$16.00)

Occasional Paper-7
Demographic Currents: Trends and Issues that Face the United States, the United Kingdom and Canada
by Richard S. Belous, with a Foreword by Thomas H.B. Symons, September 1991 (£5.00, U.S.$8.00)

Occasional Paper-6
Man and His Environment
by the late Harry G. Johnson, with a Commentary by Frances Cairncross, June 1990 (£5.00, U.S.$8.00)

Publications of the BNAC

Publications of the British-North American Committee are available from:

In Great Britain and Europe
BRITISH-NORTH AMERICAN RESEARCH ASSOCIATION
Grosvenor Gardens House
35-37 Grosvenor Gardens
London SW1W 0BS

Tel: 071-828 6644
Fax: 071-828 5830

In the United States of America
NATIONAL PLANNING ASSOCIATION
1424 16th Street NW, Suite 700
Washington, DC 20036

Tel: 202-884 7623
Fax: 202-797 5516

In Canada
C.D. HOWE INSTITUTE
125 Adelaide Street East
Toronto, Ontario M5C 1L7

Tel: 416-865 1904
Fax: 416-865 1866